MW00488673

A TIME

to

HEAL

HOW ONE SURGEON'S RELENTLESS OBEDIENCE
TO GOD BROUGHT HEALING
TO HUNDREDS OF THOUSANDS—
AND TO HIMSELF.

SCOTT HARRISON, M.D.

FOUNDER OF CURE INTERNATIONAL AND ORTHOPEDIC SURGEON

1837 CABIN PUBLISHING

Cover Design by Jeanette Gillespie, Jam Graphic Design
Interior Design by Beth Shagene
Edited by David Lambert for Somersault

Manufactured in the United States of America

17 18 19 20 21 22 • 19 18 17 16 15 14 13 12 11 10 9 8 7 6 5 4 3 2 1

Dedicated to Ann Louise Harrison,
killed at twenty-six years of age while serving
the Hmong tribal people of northern Thailand.

﹋

CONTENTS

Foreword 7

Acknowledgments 11

PART 1: JUST A LITTLE PATCH OF ICE

1. Dodging a Bullet? 15
2. Depression? Alzheimer's? Brain Tumor?
   Something Else? 21
3. Post-Concussion Syndrome 27

PART 2: THE CURE

4. Turning Point 37
5. Manyoro—and the Germ of an Idea 51
6. CURE Is a Reality! 71
7. A Clinic in Afghanistan 83
8. CURE—Walking the Walk 97

PART 3: A LIFETIME OF SURGERY

9. Vietnam 109
10. Lewis 133
11. Kipkoeck 159
12. Miss Modesty and the Arrival of AIDS 175
13. Face-to-Face with My Own Mortality 191

PART 4: COMING TO TERMS WITH IMPAIRMENT

14. From Paranoia to Alienation 205
15. Final Healing 213

Epilogue: The Final Step 231

Foreword

SOMETIMES YOU MEET SOMEONE AND KNOW THEY ARE GOING
to change your life. In 2000, at the start of the new century in the
East End of London, where my family originates, my wife, Vicky,
and I met Scott Harrison and his wife, Sally, for dinner at a small
restaurant in Hackney called Boulevards.

I had been working as an orthopedic surgeon in Malawi for
the last four years, and we were home in UK for a short break
for the birth of our third son, Timmy. Malawi is small and very
poor, and for much of my time there I was the only orthopedic
surgeon in the country. Toward the end of 1999 I had a dream of
building a Christian children's orthopedic hospital. Somewhere
kids with crippling conditions like severe bow legs, untreated
club feet, and twisted spines, kids whose bodies needed straight-
ening up, could come for surgery in an atmosphere of love, a
place where they were the center of attention. This dream had
been lingering in my mind for months when by chance I heard
of Scott Harrison and the hospital he had set up in Kenya and
the two he was setting up in Uganda and Tanzania. I had not yet
met Scott, but here was someone who not only shared my dream
but had fulfilled it several times over. At a surgical conference

in Kenya, I took the opportunity to visit the children's hospital that Scott had started at Kijabe. It was beautiful, situated on the edge of the Great Rift Valley with stunning views and cool breezes. It was spotlessly clean and had a friendly, attentive staff, but what impressed me most was that it was efficient; five to ten children would pass through its theaters each day and undergo a mini-miracle in which their limbs and spines were straightened and corrected. I saw groups of boisterous, laughing children learning to walk again on their newly straightened limbs, with their mobility, their independence, their pride, and their lives restored. I wanted to build a hospital like this.

I had found a site, I had identified funds, I had identified staff, I had even chatted with the Minister of Health, but I had no experience in building a hospital. In Scott Harrison, I had found a man who had built several hospitals in the USA and was on his third in Africa.

I remember every detail of that first meeting with Scott Harrison: his monogrammed shirt, his expensive jacket, his firm and decisive manner, and his purposeful approach to life. I had met a hero.

Scott and Sally became dear friends that night in Hackney, and although we are often separated by oceans, we have walked many paths together over the past seventeen years.

These memoirs tell the story of a man who has done more than any other person alive to help disabled children in resource-poor countries who need life-changing surgery. Scott is a surgeon, and he writes like a surgeon, using the pen as he would use a scalpel—carefully, skillfully, and purposefully.

There are four main strands to the book. First there is the story of the birth of CURE and its astonishing growth to become the world's biggest Christian children's orthopedic mission.

Second, there is Scott and Sally's own journey to faith, a journey taken at the top of a professional and business career, and the response to their newfound faith of a husband and wife who had everything the world could offer, unselfishly giving their wealth and their skills back to God. Third, there is the story of Scott's head injury and its effect on his memory, concentration, relationships, and work, told with the experience of a man who knows the intimate structure of the human body, a man whose time in Vietnam had shown him the catastrophic effects of injury to the brain. Finally, there is a story of reconciliation. I walked with Scott and Sally through this period when the organization they created shut its doors to them. Those doors have now opened, and with tears, hugs, and handshakes, Scott and Sally have been reunited with what they have labored so long, so faithfully, and with such great sacrifices to build.

If I had to choose only one word to sum up the purpose of life on earth, of our relationship with God and our relationships with other people, I would choose *reconciliation*. This book ends with a moving and personal account of reconciliation by a man I feel proud to call my friend and brother.

Professor Chris Lavy OBE MD, MCh, FRCS
Professor of Orthopaedics and Tropical Surgery
Oxford University
Oxford, England

Acknowledgments

Healing, both spiritual and physical, is God's act of love to those in need, and for that I am and will always be grateful.

My partner in this journey has been Sally; wife, co-worker, confidante, encourager, instructor, best friend, and love of my life. None of these healings, medical or spiritual, would have happened without the foundation of prayer that she created and nurtured.

I owe thanks and gratitude...

To Dave Lambert, my editor at Somersault, a special thanks for separating the wheat from the chaff and doing it with kindness.

To the other specialists at Somersault: Jeannette Taylor, Cindy Lambert, and Joe Sherman, many thanks.

To Chris Lavy, whose passion for the disabled children of Africa was inspirational.

To Jim Cohick, who was instrumental in building our first hospital and creating the template for the next dozen, and to Lynn Harrison Cohick for graciously putting your career on hold to facilitate that.

To my son Chris, whose encouragement as we built that first hospital was so helpful.

To Rex Lysinger, the first chairman of CURE International, who brought a gravitas of professionalism to our work.

To David Hungerford, MD, whose expertise as an orthopedic surgeon and clinician insured the highest level of professionalism among our surgeons and nurses.

To the first Board members of CURE International: in addition to Rex and David, Jerry Tubergen, Ed Stillman, Peter Schultz, Denis Schloser, Marilyn Quayle, John Temple, Bill Goodwyn, Sandy Lamb, Joe Olshefski, Judy Bellig, Keith Kelly.

To the current president of CURE, Roger Spoelman.

To Nardos Bekele-Thomas, who along with her husband Tunde made the Ethiopian hospital possible.

To Ralph Doudera, who was generous when CURE was still mainly a dream.

To Doug and Marcia Lanaha, who brought healing to Niger's disabled children.

To Gordon Loux, who knew just the right people at just the right time.

To Tom Coffman, who helped guide us when there was no clear path.

To Craig Hammon, who generated the funds when CURE was in its most rapid growth phase.

And to Ben Warf, MD, who met the challenge of saving the lives of thousands and thousands of children with hydrocephalus through the development of an innovative, inexpensive surgical procedure that could be taught to doctors who lacked neurosurgical training.

PART 1

JUST A LITTLE PATCH OF ICE

CHAPTER 1

DODGING A BULLET?

WHETHER I'M STARTING THIS BOOK AT THE BEGINNING—OR at the beginning of the end—depends on your perspective.

‿

I saw the sheet of ice glistening in the afternoon sun a half second too late.

Out of control, my skis veered sharply in different directions as soon as they accelerated from the heavy, moist spring snow onto the ice. One ski pole rotated over my head like a helicopter rotor, then slipped off my glove and away. The other pole vaulted me skyward as it bit into the hoar-frost and stuck fast.

One often hears people say that at life-changing moments everything goes into slow motion. But for a skier, a routine fall on the slopes seldom seems like a life-changing moment when it's happening. Falls occur all the time. And this one happened all too quickly, not in slow motion. I was aware of a flash of self-loathing for having not seen this treacherous sheet of ice, then a cruel jolt as I smashed onto the ice, then—quiet.

Central Pennsylvania, where I live, has lots of terrain that some locals refer to as mountains, although—sorry, Pennsylvanians—they barely qualify as foothills. One such hill that I can see from my bedroom window has a dozen or so ski slopes. Most are gentle intermediate ballrooms that encourage wide, sweeping turns, ideal for beginners—or orthopedic surgeons in their seventies. My home is only ten minutes away from those slopes, and if I go before school lets out, I have them to myself. It isn't Rocky Mountain powder. It's Appalachian ice and slush. But in early 2011, it was that or no skiing.

So on that early March midweek afternoon, I was recapturing the exhilaration of wide, gliding turns through gleaming snow crystals, the chatter of my skis, and a softly hummed Viennese waltz accompanying my dancing. Patches of sparkling, treacherous ice gleamed, but alone on the hill I had the freedom to dance around them. *One,* two, three; *one,* two, three … the shadow of a hawk's aerial ballet flashed across the snow in front of me.

And then the ice and the fall.

I found myself splayed face down on the ice. My skis formed a cross over my motionless body, my arms spread as if to embrace the slope.

I fought off grogginess, then groped for my helmet, which was no longer on my head. My hair felt wet as I put it back on. Water, I assumed.

I sat up, confused. Where had all these people suddenly come from? Seconds earlier, I had been the only one on the slope. Now I was surrounded by maybe a dozen skiers.

"Don't move, sir. The ski patrol will be here any minute," one said.

"We sent someone to get them," said another, looking anxious.

"I'm fine. I don't need any help. Would you get me that pole?" I said, trying to reorient myself as I struggled shakily to my feet.

"They're bringing a toboggan to get you off the hill," another onlooker said.

"I don't need to be carried off!" I said, grabbing the other pole from the reluctant hand of one of the skiers. "I'm fine!"

"Don't go, please!" another shouted. "You ..."

But by that time, I was too far down the hill to hear what he was trying to tell me.

Still groggy and with a pounding headache, I made it down to the empty ski lift and rode it to the slope leading to the parking lot. *Where did all those people come from—and so quickly? I wondered. And what was all that about sending for a toboggan to take me off the ski slope?*

Skiing onto the parking lot, I noticed people staring at me. One look in my truck's sideview mirror explained why: My face was covered in blood. So was my parka.

My temple was still throbbing as I pulled into our driveway several minutes later. My wife, Sally, a nurse, was accustomed to blood—just not on her husband's face and not in that amount. Deciding to spare her that, I went through the side door into the kitchen, where I ditched the bloody parka and washed the blood from my face.

I checked myself in the nearby bathroom mirror. There. Presentable again. No harm, no foul.

⤶

My headaches lasted ten days. OK, maybe two weeks. Well, OK, three, but barely perceptible that third week. Over those three weeks I noticed that I was also a little edgy, constantly frustrated, and frequently agitated—not so much about what people did but about what I thought they *might* do. So, admittedly, I was a little paranoid, but I had a ready and credible explanation for that. There were a lot of things going on in my life that were emotionally painful, hard to deal with. Why *wouldn't* I be a little paranoid?

Still, at least I'd dodged one bullet. The blow to my head on the ski slopes had come to nothing.

Or so I thought.

A few months later, I kept my annual appointment with my internist, Jim Rich—a friend of twenty years. "How're things?" he asked casually as he walked into the examining room.

To my surprise, I began to rant. "How are things?" I repeated. "How would you expect? I can't sleep, for one thing. And small wonder—everything seems to be going wrong. And everything seems to bother me these days! And why not? My equilibrium's off, especially at night—my balance is terrible. I feel like an old man." I had a ringing in my ears too, of all things, but I didn't bother to mention that. I was well aware that I was already sounding like a crotchety whiner.

Even so, I couldn't stop. "And to top it off, my memory's going. I can't remember the simplest things, things that a few weeks ago I'd have been able to recall in an instant. I almost got lost on the way to your office! As a doctor, I'm afraid that the likely diagnosis is all too clear. Early senility, I suppose. It may even be ... well, you know." I couldn't bring myself to say the "A" word. Loss of my memory would, I expected, be followed by loss of my other mental faculties. I would be wetting myself in a few years and not even know it!

My doctor calmly asked several more questions, both general and specific, and then sat back, considered, and said something that surprised me. "You're not losing your memory," he said. "You're suffering from depression. No surprise there. After all these years, you're retiring from the nonprofit you and Sally created and have shaped, carried, and served for so long in countries around the world. You're stepping away from the ministry that has given your life shape and meaning for sixteen years. You're retiring from CURE. Small wonder you're depressed."

I winced. "Depressed? Really?" I didn't think I was depressed.

As it turned out, I was to get much worse news than that. About the way I would leave CURE.

And about the damage to my head.

CHAPTER 2

DEPRESSION? ALZHEIMER'S? BRAIN TUMOR? SOMETHING ELSE?

I RECENTLY SAW THE MOVIE *CONCUSSION* STARRING ACTOR Will Smith. In it, he plays Doctor Bennet Omalu, a forensic pathologist who was one of the first doctors who identified a condition known as CTE (chronic traumatic encephalopathy). He was encouraged in this work by Cyril Wecht, MD, a world renowned forensic pathologist and a professor at my medical school, the University of Pittsburgh. Watching the movie reminded me of an occasion when, as president of the Student Medical Society, I was introducing Dr. Wecht as the keynote speaker to about six hundred students and faculty. As I recited his many honors and accomplishments, I realized that I could not remember his name—a not unusual problem for me. It was either Cyril Wecht or Cecil Shepps. I bailed out with, "Needing no further introduction, let me welcome our speaker." I nodded to whoever he was and walked off the stage.

That was humorous and inconsequential. But his support in confirming the then "invisible" changes in the brain after trauma was part of the breakthrough that has revolutionized our thinking of single or repeated brain trauma. Football players are at risk because of the concussions or even just repeated blows to the head suffered during their years in the National Football League. Boxers are also vulnerable. There is a continuum of brain dysfunction caused by blows to the head, creating repeated blunt brain trauma that results in physical concussion and eventually to the anxieties, erratic behavior, and, all too often, suicide in professional soldiers. It continues in every war; it is just known by different names. I saw it in Vietnam. It's estimated that as many as 30 percent of the combat soldiers in any conflict return with post-traumatic psychological impairment. It is now an epidemic, and the associated suicides make it the leading cause of death in our war against terrorism.

But at the time I had this discussion with my doctor, even just those few years ago, much less was being said about it. Even though the two of us had nearly ninety years of collective medical experience and knew that I'd had a significant blow to the head not long before, a traumatic brain injury with its neurological and psychological sequelae wasn't the first thought for either of us.

"Actually," I told my doctor after he suggested depression as the cause of my symptoms, "I'm not depressed. Sure, I have lots of feelings about the changes looming in my life. Frustrations, maybe. But depression? Nope. That's not one of them."

When he looked at me with a hint of skepticism, I said, "I know about founderitis, that pseudo-psychosis that people who start successful companies get when they retire." My voice sounded a bit louder than necessary. "And I'm proud of founding CURE. I have every right to be. It has grown from nothing to be a $123 million nonprofit that saves children's lives around the world! But can I walk away? Absolutely. I've done my bit."

He sat quietly a moment, looking at me. "Depression can take different forms," he said—patronizingly, I thought. "There's a battery of psychological tests I'd like to give you. And I'll be very surprised if they don't demonstrate that, despite what you think, you are indeed depressed. And," he added, "I'm going to test your memory too. Just to be sure."

His exam, which included a complete physical as well as the psychological tests, took an hour and a half. The memory test was last. "There will be thirty items on the test," he said. "In addition, remember these three numbers: 5, 19, 12. I'll ask you to repeat them later."

I tried to figure out a retention anchor to hold those three numbers in my mind, but couldn't think of one. Still, twenty minutes later when he asked me what they were, I lucked out: 5, 19 … uh, 12. He tried it once more as we concluded, and again I was able to reel them off.

"Congratulations!" he said. "You're the first person I've given this test to who didn't miss a single one of the questions. So I can assure you: You're not losing your memory—or your mind."

I was surprised how relieved I was to hear him say it. But was he right—or was this just his version of psychotherapy?

"I also want to check to be sure that there's no cortical atrophy," he said, "given that you're seventy-four. I'll order a CT of your brain. As I remember, you had one five years ago. Was it a fall from one of your horses that time? Anyway, it was normal."

I hope I don't forget to get the scan, I thought as I left his office.

A few weeks later, I reported for the CT scan. The technician who explained the procedure looked familiar, so I wasn't surprised when she said, "I did your scan five years ago. Would you like a copy of the scan when we're done?" I told her that I would.

Afterward, she showed me back to the waiting area. "I'll have that report printed in a minute," she said with a smile.

Nice lady, I thought. I picked up a year-old copy of *Sports Illustrated* and thumbed aimlessly through outdated predictions about the NFL season long finished. *Wrong on most of those predictions,* I thought. I tossed the magazine back onto the table. *Wonder what's keeping her.*

Just then she reappeared—but she wasn't smiling this time, and her face seemed flushed. "I've called Dr. Rich with the report. He said he'd meet you at his office as soon as you can get there to discuss it with you."

She didn't offer me a copy! And Jim would be waiting at his office to discuss it with me? As a doctor myself, I knew exactly what this kind of tiptoeing around implied. *Brain tumor!* What else could be so bad that she wouldn't tell me? It couldn't be a congenital anomaly—that would have shown up on the scan I'd had five years before. *Well,* I thought, *at least I've had enough time to get CURE up and running ... and nearly enough time to pass it on into good hands.*

Dr. Rich's office was five minutes away. The waiting room was empty except for an overweight woman, clearly distressed, who looked up at me and started talking, eager for an audience. "I walked all the way over from Harrisburg. It took two hours!" Her blouse was soaked with perspiration. "Now they tell me I got my day wrong. I was supposed to come tomorrow." She paused, then said, "I have sugar!"

She waited then, as if expecting me to tell her my problem, as worried patients often do in waiting rooms everywhere.

I wondered: *Should I tell her that I probably have a brain tumor? Or that I can't seem to handle leaving an organization I've founded and put every ounce of blood, sweat, and tears into ... oh yeah, and about $30 million of our life savings?* I seemed to be more confused than she was.

The office nurse interrupted my thoughts with the dreaded words, "The doctor will see you now." Then she turned to the anxious woman. "Another doctor will see you shortly," she said.

"Have a seat," Jim said, nodding toward a well-worn chair that had supported many anxious patients. He got right to the point. "You have a subdural hematoma. It's in the left parietal region, the same side where you had the scalp laceration some months back. It looks like it's resolving. It's the size of a golf ball. Perhaps when acute it was more like a tennis ball. You had additional hemorrhaging in the surrounding brain tissue as well, but we'd need fancier studies to show that more clearly. It's now morphing into a chronic subdural, likely permanent … but you can live with it. The need for surgery is unlikely."

It was one more piece falling into place in a puzzle that had been bothering me for weeks. "Jim, that fall on the ski slope in March—I'll tell you what I haven't told anyone else. I keep obsessing about that fall. There was a period of time—maybe seven or eight minutes, maybe ten—that I can't account for." I shook my head. "I would swear there was no one on that slope when I fell. And then suddenly I was surrounded! I must have been lying there unconscious for several minutes to have attracted a crowd of skiers that size. And that would explain why they all seemed so concerned, and why they had called the ski patrol to bring a stretcher!"

"You had a severe concussion, Scott—that much is certain. The CT suggests that the greatest injury was to the parietal area of your brain, but that hematoma put pressure on *all* of your brain." He looked at me soberly. "You're lucky to be alive, Scott. And you understand why. Remember from med school, the *contrecoup* injury? With sudden deceleration of the head, like you hitting solid ice, the brain is injured not just at the point of impact but also 180 degrees from the primary blow by a rebound effect. You had that as well. Mortality rates for acute subdurals range from 30 to 60 percent! This was a significant injury to your brain, and it probably explains your depression and other symptoms. But you seem to be getting better. Friend, you dodged a bullet. Let's follow up in a year."

Here was my doctor, a good friend, telling me that I'd been in danger but that I was going to be OK. I was glad he thought so.

I wasn't so sure.

CHAPTER 3

POST-CONCUSSION
SYNDROME

Jim got it half right.

It would be months before I knew the complete diagnosis.

I was one of thousands, make that tens of thousands, who've had a traumatic brain injury (TBI) that went unrecognized and was undertreated. After all, there was no definitive blood test enabling doctors to make that diagnosis. And even now, a few years later and with all of the publicity that has accompanied the prevalence of traumatic closed-head brain injuries among football players and veterans returning from conflicts in the Middle East, we are just beginning to see sophisticated diagnostic studies that could, had they been performed on me soon after my injury, have shown the physical damage in my brain.

But that didn't happen. So at the time of Jim's diagnosis of my chronic subdural hematoma, neither of us mentioned antidepressant medication. Neither of us mentioned cognitive therapy. The CT scan had revealed the physical damage to my brain: the formation of a blood-filled mass, initially perhaps about the size of a tennis ball, which had put pressure on my brain and suggested the possibility of hemorrhaging within the substance of the brain itself. What was just as important, if not more so, was what the CT *wasn't* able to show: the damage to my individual brain cells and the associated impaired mental processing, as demonstrated by my changed behavior. But I shouldn't be too hard on Jim; doctors have undertreated brain injuries for centuries.

That brain injury in March of 2011 was a turning point in my life. Despite my doctor's belief that I was OK and functioning normally outside of some depression, I had lost some important cognitive skills. I knew something was wrong—I just didn't know what it was. And because those cognitive skills were the very ones I needed to recognize my decreased cognitive ability, I was ill equipped to figure it out. And that's the problem faced by those who, like me, have experienced TBIs that have resulted in cognitive and emotional dysfunction. We're on the inside looking out. We can't see ourselves as others see us or hear ourselves as others hear us. While others around me might have been able to observe and even describe my changed behaviors and attitudes, I was behaving in ways that, at the time, seemed perfectly reasonable and appropriate to me. Of *course* I was furious about what so-and-so did—who wouldn't be? Of *course* I suspected that everyone was conspiring against me behind my back—because (at least to my warped perception) they were! To others I seemed paranoid, or overreactive, or overly sensitive. But to me, I was simply responding in the most appropriate way to a difficult set of circumstances.

Even so, I knew something had been wrong with me since the fall on the ice, and it was still wrong.

Life-changing events affect us in two different ways, depending on the nature of the event. Most of them are easy to recognize. Such things as the death of a loved one, a divorce, or on a more positive note, being accepted into medical school, are events we immediately recognize, both intellectually and emotionally, as ones that will leave us in some way forever changed. At other times, we're so wrapped up in the circumstances that only afterward do we grasp how much they affected us—and that is especially true when the event is accompanied by physical injury. At those times we may realize only much later, after our physical recovery, how drastically those events changed our lives.

Long before my fall on the ice, I had begun to plan my departure from CURE International, the medical ministry my wife, Sally, and I had founded and shaped (which I will describe more fully in part 2 of this book). Yes, leaving CURE would be an immense change in my life. But my track record for making major changes gave me confidence that I could handle the transitions. After all, I was, and always had been, "pathologically optimistic."

Early in my medical career, leaving my first orthopedic group to launch a solo practice—no problem! I knew I could make it on my own.

Twenty years later, leaving my practice, which had by that time grown to a seven-doctor group—leaving in fact the practice of orthopedics altogether to take on the challenge of orchestrating the recovery of a failing orthopedic manufacturing company—no problem! I'm sure others wondered what I'd been smoking. After all, my orthopedic practice was successful in every way, and several experienced CEOs had already looked at the orthopedic manufacturer, shaken their heads, and walked away. Not me! Mister Optimist said, "We can turn this failing company around!" And we did. Four years later, we sold it for three times what it had been worth when I stepped in.

So why should leaving CURE throw me for a loop? Why, after the injury, did my behavior and my feelings about leaving the nonprofit become more and more irrational, extreme, and puzzling to everyone around me?

To put it simply, after the traumatic brain injury, I wasn't playing with a full deck. But I didn't realize it. Or to use professional lingo, I was experiencing the patho-psychological sequelae of a significant head injury with intracranial hemorrhage and a subsequent subdural hematoma, about twice the size that usually requires immediate surgical decompression. (That's doctor-speak for being a little crazy and a little slow from severe brain trauma.)

My brain *had* been injured; the CT showed that. But the new generation of diagnostic tools like positron emission tomography (PET) and diffusion tensor imaging (DTI), neither of which was performed on me, could have quantified the damage and alerted me that I was now seeing the world differently. Even more sophisticated research studies that are now available could have identified, down to the last millimeter, exactly which area of brain cells had been killed or damaged.

Those tests, had they been performed, would have led to the diagnosis of post-concussion syndrome from a traumatic brain injury. In retrospect it seems clear, a classic case. But to arrive at that answer, we would have had to ask the right questions—and no one was asking them.

Shouldn't I—a trained doctor with many years of experience—have been asking those questions, given that, after all, I was the one experiencing the symptoms? Well, yes—except that, again, I was on the inside looking out. It stands to reason that if your symptoms are mental ones, you may not be thinking clearly enough to reliably evaluate the implications of those symptoms, regardless of your level of training and knowledge. After all, I told myself, I was in my midseventies and doing a job that would have been demanding for a fifty-year-old. Add to that the stress of stepping down from the ministry that meant so much to me, and I thought I had adequate explanation for my symptoms. Who wouldn't be a bit on edge under those circumstances?

It has become almost an aphorism: The crazy person never thinks he's crazy. I wasn't crazy—but I wasn't completely sane either, given the symptoms I was experiencing.

Imagine a Special Forces soldier who sustains a closed-head injury when a roadside bomb explodes in Afghanistan or Iraq. Regular X-rays are taken of his head back at the base hospital—and they look normal, even though in fact that marine experienced a soft-tissue injury in the substance of his brain. That's because a "bruise" within the brain tissue, somewhat like the black-and-blue mark on your arm or leg muscle when you get a bruise there, doesn't show up on regular X-rays. It takes more sophisticated diagnostic tests to show those changes within the brain tissue. I had that type of damage.

I also had (as that soldier might have had as well) bleeding within the potential space that covers the brain, i.e., the subdural space. One side is bordered by the rigid bony skull covered by a strong membrane, the periosteum. That bone isn't going to give unless fractured. On the other side, this potential space is bordered by the dura, a membrane covering the soft tissue of the brain. When bleeding in the brain occurs, some of the blood may collect in this potential space inside the dura, compressing the softer brain tissue and thereby interfering with the functioning of that portion of the brain. That's why as many as half of the victims of acute subdural bleeding die.

The symptoms of the compression of the brain tissue by that subdural blood clot are similar to those of a concussion but usually much worse.

So, whether for the unfortunate skier who falls and slams his head onto the unforgiving ice or for the Special Forces soldier injured by an IED in Afghanistan or Iraq, three injuries happen in rapid succession. First, there's an impact concussion to the brain cells, injuring some permanently and others temporarily. Second, a mass forms in the subdural space between the bony skull and the underlying brain, which compresses and injures, even kills, yet more brain cells. Finally, the patient, if still alive, has a psychological response to the physical changes in his brain. In other words, his emotions and probably also his behavior change, and that change is almost always negative.

Recently there has been an explosion of interest in brain injuries of this type. This comes in part from an increased awareness of the number of veterans returning from service in Afghanistan and Iraq who have received TBIs from concussive blasts of high explosives. We think of this as something new, a result of our country's war on terror, but in truth the incidence of injuries of this type stretches back to the invention of gunpowder. If it seems that they have increased in more recent conflicts, it may be because the state of medical care has improved to the point that many more victims of such attacks are surviving long enough for the effects of their brain injuries to manifest in their behavior.

Surprisingly, not all veterans of Iraq and Afghanistan who exhibit these symptoms sustained head injuries. They exhibit symptoms similar to post-concussion syndrome but without the head trauma.

It was called shell shock in World War I and battle fatigue in World War II, but let's be honest—many thought of it as coward-ice. "Combat stress reaction" we called it when soldiers returning from Vietnam exhibited it. Many of those Vietnam veterans are still wandering the streets and passing through homeless shelters or mental institutions, through no fault of their own. What all of these soldiers have in common, regardless of the war they fought in, are many of the symptoms of post-concussion syndrome (PCS) without the component of physical injury—at least as far as such injury is diagnosable with current testing. We have a new name for their condition: post-traumatic stress disorder, or PTSD, an epidemic that affects 20 percent of combat soldiers returning from Afghanistan and the Middle East to a home where they no longer feel safe or accepted, and to loved ones who barely recognize them. It's a massive problem that is overwhelming medical resources.

But it's not only in the military that injuries like mine are being noticed because of their devastating effect. As depicted in the Will Smith movie *Concussion,* mentioned earlier, a great deal of attention is being given to the head injuries occurring in sports, especially American football, that are very similar to those we're seeing in our returning veterans. PCS can result from a single severe concussion, such as that received from a road-side bomb in Iraq, or it can result from multiple smaller injuries to the brain, as from scores of headfirst collisions with three-hundred-pound linemen, even when wearing a "protective" helmet and even if each individual collision didn't have an immediate noticeable effect.

Why the syndrome occurs in some injury victims and not others remains a mystery. For some, the deleterious effects occur quickly, while for others the onset is delayed by decades. The severity of the concussion (they're classified as grades 1, 2, or 3; mine was a 3, the worst) is often an indicator of the likelihood of the occurrence of PCS, but not in all cases. Headache, nausea, dizziness, fatigue, sleep disorders, drowsiness, irritability, anxiety, depression, mood swings, a sense of sadness, and difficulty concentrating or remembering are some of the most common symptoms. That's a lot of symptoms to sort through, which can complicate diagnosis; fortunately, seldom does any one patient have all of them.

In my case, my concussion left me unconscious for perhaps eight to ten minutes and gave me enough of these symptoms that they should have triggered suspicion of a concussion. But my internist—well, he acted like an internist, not a neurosurgeon, a sports medicine doc, or even a psychiatrist. As a result, he flat-out missed the diagnosis. I can't blame him—it had been a long time since he'd taken a call in an ER on a Saturday night and attended patients with TBIs resulting from bottles crashing over skulls or heads bursting through car windshields.

And let's be fair, I'm a doctor and I hadn't diagnosed it either!

However it happened, I had lost something I'd taken for granted all my life: my ability to correctly interpret the world I lived in. It's an experience I share with many of our soldiers as well as many of our sports heroes. It's a lot more common than we think. And it can happen to people in many ways.

In my case, it threatened my ability to orchestrate my own departure from the ministry that meant so much to my wife and me, the ministry we had founded so many years before in Africa: CURE International.

PART 2

THE CURE

CHAPTER 4

Turning Point

"There's something I have to tell you," Sally said nervously one evening. "About something … something I've done." We were both standing in the kitchen. I had just come home in time for my customary late dinner. Her words caught me in the middle of taking off my coat, and I froze with one arm out, one arm in. It wasn't just what she had said. It was also that she was nervously rubbing her hands, something I did not recall ever seeing her do before.

"I think I know what it is," I said. "This happened about ten days ago, right?"

She looked puzzled. "What do you mean?"

"Well," I said, "when I went to work that morning, you were one person, and when I came home that night, you were somebody else. You've always been one of the nicest people I know— no, make that the nicest. But that evening I sensed something different. I couldn't define it—a sense of tranquility, yes, but also great vitality. You gave off a quietude and beauty I could sense but not put into words. In spite of the bedlam of a house full of teenagers, you had a tender serenity—subtle but new. And a new strength."

I thought I knew what had happened because of something Sally and I had often discussed. This was, after all, the midseventies, the era when convicted Watergate conspirator Chuck Colson said he'd been "born again"—and had even written a book by that title. A peanut farmer from Georgia named Jimmy Carter was running for president; he too said he was "born again." What was all that supposed to mean?

Though neither Sally nor I had experienced it, we'd been talking about what it might be, what being born again might mean. We'd begun dating as teenagers while attending the local Methodist church's youth fellowship. Our conclusion had always been that it was intriguing but not something for us. But Sally had recently met a woman in a Bible study who seemed to radiate the presence of Christ and yet made no overt attempt to proselytize.

Then, on a September morning in 1976, after I had gone to work and the kids had left for school, Sally had simply and quietly asked Christ to come into her life and become personal to her, become Lord of her life. She had begun that prayer as one person and finished it a different person. But she had refrained from telling me until she was sure that it was real. Now it was ten days later and she had no doubt. The time had come.

"Really? You saw the change?" she said with a smile. "I've been wondering since that day, how can I explain this spiritual change inside me? I *knew* it was real, I could feel it … and now you say you saw it too."

As a doctor, I'd been trained as a scientist. This phenomenon that we had often discussed and that now my wife was claiming to have experienced didn't fit smoothly into my technically oriented mind; it definitely lay outside my area of expertise. But I loved Sally, and although I didn't understand it, I couldn't dispute what she had experienced. But was this "born-again" thing really the gateway to God? I wasn't convinced. I kept looking for loopholes.

That search for loopholes wasn't new; it dated all the way back to the summer I was twelve, when my parents sent me off to Methodist church camp in the mountains of western Pennsylvania. Up on a nearby ridge was a massive steel cross. When the floodlights came on at night, it could be seen from miles around.

The third day of camp, the luncheon speaker made a fever-pitch challenge to all of us to give control of our lives to Jesus. A few of my newfound friends jumped up from their seats at the dining table and went forward. Then more of them. Eventually, I looked around to see that most of the seats in the dining hall were empty.

But I stayed put. Did I really want to give total control of my life to this itinerant preacher I'd heard about in Sunday school? Things were going pretty well in my life. I wasn't the best guy on our basketball team, but I was probably the second best. I was making good grades. I was working at Dad's store and making some money. I even had a girlfriend, the prettiest girl in fifth grade. So why risk losing all that for some historical person named Jesus?

If you've been to Christian summer camp, you know what happens on the last night of camp. We all headed up the mountain for a bonfire near that mammoth cross. Besides the light from the bonfire, floodlights illuminated the cross. As the speaker gave his talk, a low cloud drifted by, and the shadow of the cross was projected on the cloud. A swell of *oohs* and *aahs* rumbled through the group sitting on the ground. "It's gotta be a sign!" somebody stage-whispered.

The speaker gave an invitation: "Everyone who wants to give their life to Jesus Christ, come forward."

It was almost as if they had played "The Star-Spangled Banner." Everybody stood up … everybody but me. I remained on the grass as the crowd of other kids shuffled past me.

Who knows—if I went up there, someday he might send me to Africa!

⌐

At the time of Sally's prayer and conversion, my career as a surgeon was nearly everything I could have hoped it to be. I was clinical professor of orthopedic surgery at the Milton S. Hershey Medical Center, the Penn State medical school that had drawn Sally's and my attention to central Pennsylvania in the first place. I loved to teach, and this was one of the few medical schools in America based in a small-town environment—a perfect combination for raising a family.

I relished sparring with medical students. It challenged me to read the orthopedic journals the day they arrived. It made my day to catch them uninformed on something. It stimulated them to read more and prepared them for when they would be sparring with malpractice lawyers.

I was also on the staff of the Elizabethtown Crippled Children's Hospital, a state facility that had a seemingly inexhaustible number of children with life-changing and life-threatening spinal deformities. I was increasingly doing the types of operations I loved. And I was on the staff of five other hospitals!

Meanwhile, I joined my friend Rocky to create the Rehab Hospital Service Corporation. To help finance it, we created a group of junior investors who were also doctors who might use the hospital. Even though we were a for-profit hospital, we charged less than the nonprofit hospitals and gave the patients better care and food. By providing quality service, our doctor/ investor team did financially very well. "Centers of excellence," we called them ... because they were! We had five facilities when we sold it to a larger hospital company in 1984.

Yes, it was almost all I could ask. Almost. There was one thing I hadn't accomplished yet that I craved. I had the respect of my peers, I had the money and the Ferrari, I had authority and power and prestige. But I did not yet belong to the Scoliosis Research Society.

To those not involved in orthopedics, that may not sound like such a big deal. Another dry scientific association. And yes, it might have been dry and academic, but it was also exclusive. Very, very exclusive! Membership then, worldwide, was one hundred and three individuals, all of them pediatric spine surgeons, all of them leaders in the field of children's reconstructive spine surgery. They came from all over the world. Most were eminent researchers or academics, and all had published numerous papers. Admission to the Scoliosis Research Society would have been an undeniable acknowledgment that I had reached the very top.

Miracle of miracles, after giving papers at their annual meetings and publishing a few on spine surgery, the membership committee, after an inquisition-level interview, finally gave me the thumbs-up. I would be inducted as the society's one hundred fourth member at its 1977 annual meeting in Hong Kong.

It can't get any better than this, I thought!

Sally and I excitedly began making plans for the trip.

As part of the junket, several American members were stopping on the way to attend the Japanese Spine Society meeting. The talks would be given in Japanese, but with English translation through headphones. As long as we were making the trip, we added this to the itinerary.

On the long flight over the Pacific, I took an informal census of the luminaries on the plane—a veritable who's who of American spine surgeons. And here I was among them, a member. I had truly made it to the next level.

The meeting was in Kyoto, the ancient imperial capital. There seemed to be a Shinto shrine on every corner. Our guide informed us that this was the birthplace of this ancient religion, which venerated ancestors. Kyoto had also originally been picked by the Americans as one of the sites to be leveled by the atomic bomb, but it was spared because of its religious history.

It didn't sound like much of a religion to me, and I couldn't quite figure out where it left off and Buddhism took over. Of course, it's also true that I would have done a pretty poor job of explaining Christianity.

The thirteen-hour time difference and untold hours in the plane left me jet-lagged. Somehow I stayed awake through the first full day of meetings. I tried to focus on the English version coming to me in translation through my headphones while attempting to shake the cobwebs from my head.

But that night, I had trouble sleeping. About four thirty in the morning, I gave up and decided to go jogging. I stumbled around the dark bedroom as quietly as I could, trying to not disturb Sally as I searched for the running shoes and shorts I had brought along. She woke up anyway. "Be sure you have the room key," she mumbled. "Don't take any money with you ... do you have your ID?"

I slipped out of the hotel and jogged down the dark streets of Kyoto, which were narrower and more cluttered than I had expected. I hadn't been running long before I stumbled over a garbage can that had, I assumed, been put out for early-morning pickup. The cacophony triggered a chorus from the neighborhood dogs. I quickly turned into a side street—where I tripped over a chain someone had rigged to delineate a parking space, and fell sprawling to the ground. I needed to find a less treacherous path, so I moved out of the residential area and found a trail up into the foothills.

Twenty-five minutes later I made the summit. The eastern sky was beginning to brighten. The city lights still twinkled at my feet. A lookout platform was silhouetted just ahead. I mounted it to better see the valley. Speckled below was a sprawl of lights, shrouded in places by a layer of morning fog. The new day was taking form.

In my personal fog, I had an odd, perhaps alien thought: The historical religion of the city below me venerated their ancestors, burning incense and candles to offer them honor and peace in their final resting places. It was natural, I suppose, that it made me think of my own father, who was at that moment taking care of Lynn, Ann, and Chris, our three children back home in Pennsylvania, freeing Sally and me to make this trip. They were probably just finishing dinner with some chocolate chip cookies or some other special treat.

I was at peace. Life was good! What more could I ask?

And yet ...

In the still silence, as the rays of the sun began to edge over the distant hills, I seemed to hear a question:

If you can trust your father to care for your children, why can't you trust me to care for you?

I heard no accusation in it. It was as if my favorite teacher was asking me a question, leading me to a new understanding ... a new answer.

I sensed it a second time: *If you can trust your father to care for your children, why can't you trust me to care for you?*

It wasn't impersonal. It was a first-person *me* who was asking. Was this the *me* who had remained, by my own choice all those long years ago and many times since, the Great Unknown in my life? Yes, I thought so. But why now? I had it all together. If I had been reluctant to grant him control over my life as a twelve-year-old at a Christian youth camp, how much more so now that I was a successful adult? I had already demonstrated, to my own satisfaction, how well life could turn out with me at the helm. Why fix what ain't broke?

I wasn't asking, *Is this all there is?* Life was good—in fact, it was very good.

But maybe that wasn't the question. Maybe I should be asking myself whether Sally, and daughters Lynn and Ann as well, had found something significant in their relationship with God—in their having been born again. Was this conceivably something I should want for myself as well? I didn't know. I struggled even to define what it was I sensed in them. A tranquil security in the love of God, perhaps? Yes. But it was more than that—way more.

And perhaps there was another question beyond that one: What would life be like if I *did* turn control of my life over to Jesus? If it was very good now, could it be even better if I took that step? I didn't know—because in truth, I really didn't "get" Christianity. In spite of growing up in the Methodist church, sitting beside Grandma Harrison every Sunday morning, I was still in the beginner class. It was a religion of paradoxes. First, Jesus, God's son, dies a humiliating death, even though he could have saved himself if he had chosen to. But we're supposed to believe that, even though he allowed himself to be tortured to death, he's in control? And capable of controlling our lives for us as well? Really!

And could I even trust the question that had started this train of thought this morning: *If you can trust your own father to care for your children, why can't you trust me, your eternal Father, to care for you?* Was that really Jesus talking to me through my thoughts, or was it just my own mental self-talk?

But wait—that was the mistake in my logic. It was hidden in the very question about my father. And now that I suddenly saw it, it seemed so obvious. It wasn't about control at all. It wasn't about power. My father wasn't devoting this time to my children because of his desire for control, to exercise power over them. He was doing it out of love.

This whole thing was about love! Not control—love!

God's desire for me to turn my life over to him was really an offer of love, just as my own father was expressing his love for my children, his joy in taking care of them. Loving them.

I wouldn't just be giving up control of my life—I would be exchanging it, trading it for the love of Jesus and, if I understood correctly, the eternal presence of the Holy Spirit.

I had known at least a tiny bit about God the Father, Son, and Holy Spirit since ... could it have been age five, when I started attending Sunday school and my mother read Bible stories to me at bedtime?

But still—what kind of sense did it make to turn my life over to God now? Don't most people have their "born again" experience when things are terrible? Wasn't Chuck Colson in jail? And the Bible is full of examples of desperate people who call out to God. There's a reason people talk about "foxhole conversions."

But I wasn't frightened or desperate! I couldn't imagine life being any better. What if, in that exchange of control for love, I ended up losing some of the things I'd worked so hard for? Precious things! Giving up control of my life to the Son of God wouldn't be a safe thing or perhaps even a wise thing to do.

If you can trust your own father to care for your children, why can't you trust me to care for you?

Was that me just thinking, or was it God's voice I was hearing? Gradually but inexorably, while marveling at the beauty of Kyoto's dawn, I went from contemplating my many blessings and accomplishments in life to feeling the love of the Son of God as he stretched out his nail-scarred hand. I reached out … paused, but just for a second … and then grasped it.

I had crossed the abyss. I was on the other side, looking back and wondering why I had waited so long to say yes. There was no doubt: I *had* crossed over the wall of disbelief, or was it fear, or perhaps just my arrogant insistence that I didn't need him. I think what I whispered next was: *Jesus, I choose to do this.* Then a bit louder, *I do trust you.* Finally, *Yes, yes, I am giving control of my life to you.*

There was no crash of thunder, no lightning bolt, no ethereal music.

There was something even better, louder, brighter, more beautiful!

His presence embracing me! Softly! Completely! Tightly!

I knew that in that moment, every fiber of my being had been changed. I was a different person. Every molecule in my body was now different. I could feel it, but it was more than emotion. It was wraithlike and ethereal, and at the same time, as practical and solid as a handshake.

I was loved by the God of the universe. Me—he loved me! In spite of my volcanic temper, my self-absorption, the impossible standards I strived for and held everyone else to … God/Jesus/ Holy Spirit loved me.

Loved me!

I was no longer afraid of what that might mean. I wasn't concerned that I would lose control.

I was loved by the God of the universe. God loved me as surely as Sally loved me.

I was loved, too, by the Son of the God of the universe, and that gave me a quiet peace.

And the Holy Spirit would be with me in this life and the next!

I had come to Japan a practical-minded surgeon-scientist, and now I stood on this hill overlooking Kyoto absolutely *ecstatic*, experiencing something as far removed from logic and practicality as possible. However this had happened, I now experienced joy beyond measure. I had a new Father and was now part of a new family, one that Sally, Lynn, and Ann already belonged to.

As the sun climbed over the horizon—had all of this really happened in only a few moments?—this forty-year-old spine surgeon finally arrived at the understanding that, despite my achievements and wealth, I would now be made happiest not by acquiring more of the same but, rather, by placing all of it on the altar for God to use as he saw fit.

Yes, *all* of it! I was all in!

Here was that Someone Else who was ultimately worthy of my honor and worship and even submission—not the ancestors who were worshiped and honored by the Shinto faith in the valley below, but rather the God who created this valley, this mountain, and everything else. And I was now deliriously in love with him.

Lord, I prayed, my mind racing, *I realize that for far too long I have refused to let you be the Lord of my life—and still you've honored and blessed me by giving me all these things: the practice, the house, the swimming pool, the sports cars, the racehorses . . . I stand amazed. And I thank you for it, but now I give it all to you—and along with it, my heart and my soul and my mind, arrogance and all!*

Then I shouted loud, "You're in charge!"

And I realized I wasn't being deprived of anything. I wasn't suddenly *less*. Instead I was putting everything I owned and had cherished into infinitely safer hands than mine. I was free. I didn't have to bear the burden of controlling and protecting all of that any more.

It wasn't even mine to worry about.

What next?

Go tell Sally!

I began running at breakneck speed down the rocky slope. *I can't wait to tell her, I can't wait to tell her!* I kept repeating, almost in cadence, as my feet bounded over the gravel path. I couldn't even feel my feet on the uneven trail. I was flying ... or was I? I was ecstatic ... bursting, overflowing, exploding with joy!

I dashed up the stairs—I had no time to wait for an elevator. Sweaty, panting, shaking, and breathless, I burst into the room. As she often did, Sally was sitting in a chair reading her Bible. She looked up expectantly.

"It's finally happened!" I said. With the words tumbling out unintelligibly, I babbled an explanation: I described jogging in the dark, falling down, deciding to run up the mountainside, looking over the city, and finally facing the ultimate question of control. I must have gone on for five minutes.

She smiled lovingly, and I'm sure I was grinning like an idiot. Once my words had run out, nothing further needed to be said. I was now home, the one my three girls lived in.

Remember Christmas morning when you were a child? You tore through all the packages in uncontrollable joy, and then suddenly it was over, and you looked around and didn't know what to do next. That's how I felt. There was nobody else on this trip we knew well enough to share such momentous news with. We had to go through the motions for another day. First I sat in medical lectures, where I couldn't focus on the content. Then there was a sightseeing tour, but as beautiful and fascinating as the city and countryside were, I was still frustrated at not being able to talk about the greatest thing that had ever happened to me— entering into this one-to-one relationship with the Son of God.

Soon we were back on the bullet train to Tokyo to catch the flight to Hong Kong. When we checked into the new hotel, we overheard people in our group complaining about their room assignments: If they faced the mountains, they wanted to face the harbor, and if they faced the harbor, they wanted to face the mountains. I had complained about the same types of inconsequential, temporal things myself many times in the past, but now, while the others were complaining, I was thinking, *Let me tell you about something that's really beautiful, really important!*

The induction ceremony into the Scoliosis Research Society was gratifying. But I knew I'd already been inducted into something greater—and eternal.

What I didn't yet know was what all of this would mean in terms of my life—I was already thinking of it as my *old* life— when we returned to Pennsylvania. Soon I would be back in Harrisburg, and although I knew my life would change in major ways, I still didn't know what those changes would be.

I did know this: I felt so much lighter now that I didn't have to carry that heavy load of control.

Later, I wondered how intimidated, and unworthy, I might have felt if God had communicated to me the whole vision of what he had in mind for me in years to come—the challenges he would set before me for what he wanted me to do, and also the changes he would need to make in me for that vision to become a reality.

I wonder what I'd have thought if he'd whispered in my ear, *There are 125,000 crippled kids in the world whom you will be instrumental in healing ... and 135,000 who will come to faith in Christ just as you have. Those you have operated on as well as their fathers, mothers, aunts, uncles, siblings, and friends will know me and, yes, be born again because of what we will be doing together.*

CHAPTER 5

Manyoro— and the Germ of an Idea

Even if God, in those early days of my faith, had shared with me a vision of a worldwide healing ministry, I would still have been dumbfounded when it happened by the ways he chose to bring it about.

In 1990, a few years after my experience in Kyoto, with my practice going extremely well, opportunities were opening up around me. Among them was a request from Kirschner Medical, the orthopedic manufacturing company on whose board I sat, that I take over leadership of the company. I sought guidance from God: "What do you want me to do with the rest of my life?" I was puzzled by the answer: *Quit your practice, accept the offer to become CEO of Kirschner, then go to Wall Street and beg for money to refinance your nearly bankrupt company.*

Not only was that not the answer I was expecting, I wasn't sure it made sense at any level. First, my practice was extremely lucrative. Not only was it providing my family with a more-than-comfortable income, but it also allowed me to donate generously to many charitable causes while at the same time helping people with serious medical needs. How did it make sense to take a big cut in pay, accepting instead a ton of stock options that might prove worthless?

Second, although I had found some success in my investments in medical business ventures, turning around a nearly bankrupt $50 million manufacturing company was a long way from managing a group of seven orthopedists. I had no idea if I had the abilities necessary to pull it off.

And third, because the time commitment I would have to make as CEO of this struggling business was 24/7, I would have to abandon the mission trips that I found so satisfying. (See my account of my first trip to Africa as a medical missionary in chapter 10.)

Making the choice to leave my practice and take charge of Kirschner would require blind obedience to God on my part—with the emphasis on *blind*.

But as is usually the case when the Lord leads us into something, he also provides the means for us to carry out his will. I followed what I sensed (from his responses to my prayers) was his leading me to become CEO of Kirschner, and four years later, after I'd invested a major part of Sally's and my savings into the company, and after we had refinanced the company to keep it afloat, we merged with one of our larger rivals, Biomet, and in so doing increased Kirschner's stock price from $3.50 per share to over $12.00.

This also meant, of course, that I had worked myself out of a job. But that was fine with me. It meant that I was once again free to ask God what he wanted next for my life—and it also meant that he had given me the financial resources to help make it happen, whatever it might be.

↬

The answer to my question came nine months later when I went to Kenya to fill in for a medical missionary. After our exhausting seventeen-hour flight, Sally and I went directly from the airport to the home of Martha, the mission hospital's nurse anesthetist, and sank into the tattered couch, grateful for a soft seat. Martha and her husband had come to the mission station forty years before. Staying on after her husband died, then ignoring the mission's policy of retirement at sixty-five, she was now seventy and had become legendary for her stamina, outworking those half her age. *Irascibly lovable* would best describe her.

Sally and I were in Kijabe, Kenya, for two reasons. First, I had picked up the phone some three or four months before to hear an American missionary doctor ask, "Would you come to Kenya and cover for me so I can attend a conference? All I do is orthopedics—right up your alley!" Then he added, "We have a mutual friend in Professor David Hungerford. He suggested I call."

Since selling Kirschner to Biomet, I had been looking to see what might be next—and that was the second reason we were in Kijabe: I had for some time been wanting to get back to Africa to test the waters about my desire to start a network of children's hospitals focused on the surgical repair of correctable disabilities. The past six years since leaving my orthopedic practice had been chaotic and exhausting, and now, even though I had agreed to come, I wondered if I would be able to resume performing surgery. The six years since I had held a scalpel seemed like a long time—long enough for fine motor skills (not to mention memory of technique, concentration, and split-second judgment) to atrophy. I intended to start small—trimming a hangnail perhaps, or draining a superficial abscess.

Maybe, I told myself, it would be like riding a bike—you never forget, and the intervening years wouldn't matter.

Sure—just like a pro golfer can take a decade off and shoot par his first time back! Yeah, right.

An intense little man wearing a large bow tie bustled in. "I'm sorry to be late for dinner," he said. "I've been stuck in the emergency room with a difficult case. A tree fell on my patient. He's paralyzed from the waist down."

He plopped down on the sofa, letting out a deep sigh. "I understand you're an orthopedist. Take a look at him in the morning if you would. Doesn't look like there's much that can to be done for him—the dislocation is at L-1 (the top vertebra in the lower back, the lumbar region). But since you're here, you might put a note on the chart to confirm his paraplegia."

The doctor in the bow tie was a general practitioner, I discovered as we chatted over dinner. His stateside hospital was only twenty minutes from my home. He reminded me that he had even sent me a patient or two before I left practice. Small world—but then, the world of stateside doctors who do short-term volunteer medical work in Africa *is* small.

Despite my jet lag, I spent a restless night thinking about that poor guy with the crushed spine. I kept imagining his future. Short, that I knew for sure. He'd be lucky to live a year, and that year would be filled with a miserable sequence of health problems. First, skin ulcers would appear, and they would lead to deeper pressure sores. The sores would soon become contaminated and infected by feces from his incontinence. And even though he had no sensation below his waist, the pain, initially from the area of dislocation and then spreading beyond, would still be excruciating. His dislocation had occurred in the lower back where the spinal cord transitions into a group of peripheral nerves that act differently from the spinal cord. At this level the tubular spinal cord transitions into a group of individual nerves which seventeenth-century anatomists called the *cauda equina*, as it looked like the tail of the horse. Those individual nerves have a greater ability to regenerate after blunt trauma than the spinal cord. They carry the impulses that reach our muscles and create motion; they also transmit pain sensation and position sense. In this case, the position of the dislocation might give this patient a slightly better chance of recovery.

Without healing, though, he would soon develop depression, anger, and bitterness. Ultimately he would alienate his family. Then sepsis would overwhelm him, and his death would be a welcome relief for everyone, especially him.

It was still dark the next morning when I left to go up to the hospital. The stars of rural Africa, undimmed by ambient light, sparkled in the dark canopy over my head. It was still too early for the African mourning dove to announce the dawn.

Kijabe is a small mission station, seven thousand feet above sea level, hanging on the eastern escarpment of the Great Rift Valley. Teddy Roosevelt, during his infamous 1911 safari with his son, stopped to lay the cornerstone on one of their first buildings.

I tried the door to the front of the hospital, but it jarred my hand. Locked! If they wanted me to work here, the least they could do was give me a key! Shaking my head, I circled around to the emergency entrance. Not much happening there either, and no one was visible. As in most emergency rooms around the world at this hour of the morning, the night-shift staff was in their hiding places, taking quick naps.

Making my way along the dimly lit corridors, I was taken aback by the smell. It wasn't the usual hospital smell, the one I'd been accustomed to for thirty-five years. There was a mustiness to it, the stench of chronic disease addressed too late with insufficient resources. It was what this injured young man had to look forward to.

It was easy for me to pick out my potential patient in the mostly dark ward; he lay with his eyes wide open and fixed on the ceiling, his dark face a rigid mask as he resolutely awaited the final verdict. Then his eyes turned to me. "Who are you?" he asked. It was more a challenge than a question. "What do you want?"

So much for gratitude for the arrival of his would-be Good Samaritan. "I'm a spine doctor from America," I said.

"Can you fix me?" he asked with that unique blend of British stiff upper lip tinged with the soft fluency of his native tongue. But his voice became shrill as, in hushed tones, he hissed, "The damn tree fell on me. I cut it down, but it didn't fall the way it should have. It nearly cut me in half. I can't feel my legs. Are they broken?"

"It's your spine that's broken … or rather, dislocated. At least that's what your doctor told me. There is a slight chance I might be able to help." I tried to sound upbeat, but even to my own ears, I failed.

His look screamed desperation.

Like nearly all Kenyans, he spoke English quite well. The story was pretty simple: He had been one of a group felling massive pine trees planted by the British occupiers fifty to sixty years before, during the country's colonial period. The tree that injured him had caromed off another smaller tree as it came crashing down, smashing into his side and instantly paralyzing him from the waist down. His friends rigged a hammock-like sling, with one bearer at each corner, and brought him out of the woods to the mission hospital. He felt no pain, but he understood that was because he felt nothing below the waist. He had been unable to create even a flicker of muscle activity in his lower body. The staining of the sheets confirmed that he had no bowel control, and the catheter draining dark cloudy urine confirmed that his bladder function was gone as well. My pin jabbing in his toe brought blood but no response.

I had only one final thing to test: Could he tell the position of his toes? I grabbed his big toe. "Where am I moving it—up or down?" I said, pushing his toe up.

"Up."

I pressed it down.

"Down," he said.

Down again. And then down again. And each time, he correctly identified the position of his toe. In fact, he identified it with 100 percent accuracy each time I asked. He still had *proprioception*, which is to say, the body's sense of where it is. No matter how bad the fracture dislocation was, the nerves of his cauda equina were at least marginally intact. That meant there was a chance, however slight, that he would not be permanently paraplegic. If we could surgically repair his dislocated spine, it would be the difference between life and death for this patient.

The question in my mind was: *Was I the surgeon who could perform that operation?* Once I had been—but getting back to delicate surgery wasn't like getting back on the proverbial bike. Ironically, about ten years previously, on my first short-term visit to southern Africa, to Malawi, I had been challenged by another spine problem, recounted in chapter 10. But at that time, I'd been doing hundreds of such procedures each year.

Returning to the nurses' station, I found the man's X-rays. His name was Manyoro—a name that was, as I would learn, common among the Kikuyu. The dislocation at the junction of the thoracic and lumbar spine was complete. The displacement at the first and second lumbar vertebrae (lower back) was so severe I couldn't believe the spinal nerves were intact. But had the injury been a couple of inches higher, Manyoro's paralysis would more likely be permanent and complete.

I returned to his room to check once again his position sense, and once again he repeated his perfect performance.

Sitting down to write the orders after so many years away from the practice of medicine, I felt as if I were back in medical school. Now, what was that acronym I'd learned to ensure that I didn't forget some vital pre-op order? My mind was blank—I couldn't remember even that! How was I going to remember the intricacies of complex spine surgery? *Doesn't matter,* I rationalized. *They probably couldn't do half of them at this hospital anyway.*

When the nurse came in, still rubbing sleep from her eyes, I began firing off orders: "He'll need four units of blood. Hold all food and fluids. The sooner we get him into the operating room, the better."

Performing a surgery of this complexity and delicacy was precisely *not* how I'd planned to start my surgical career comeback. *I may flame out before I ever get started,* I thought. But that concern sounded petty compared to the possibility of giving this man a chance at a normal life, or *any* life, for that matter.

The operating room was just coming to life as I entered, introduced myself, and asked to see the spinal instruments and equipment. This request was met with embarrassed laughter. But then one of the old-timers remembered a corner in a back closet containing some bewildering "stuff." "It's just the junk that has accumulated over the years from the visiting docs," she explained, guiding me to the closet.

As I sorted through the discarded orthopedic equipment, I

decided that she was right to call it junk. I found a few screws of varying length, a scratched metal plate designed for a fractured tibia, and a couple of spools of wire. It was a far cry from the stainless steel surgical sets I'd taken for granted in the States. Wouldn't I love to have found some titanium pedicle screws, laminar hooks, vertebral rods—all the things that would restore stability to this young man's spine!

What was my new patient's name again? Manyoro! "Well, Manyoro, this isn't going to be pretty," I mumbled to no one in particular, starting back toward the OR. "You're going to get surgery with inadequate equipment, an inexperienced surgical assistant (I had recruited a missionary general surgeon practicing at the hospital to help me, but he kept reminding me that he'd never assisted in a spinal operation), and a questionably competent orthopedist. But it's the only shot you're going to get."

And I'll pray for you, I thought. *Really, really hard!*

It would take the staff a few hours to sterilize the equipment I'd resurrected from the junk box. Further bad news: They could get only half the blood I'd ordered. "If we run into trouble," I warned them, "this could be a blood-spattered three-to-four-hour operation." *Not to mention*, I thought, *that I'm not sure I'll even know which end of the scalpel to hold, much less be able to manage complex reconstructive surgery.*

I went home for a late breakfast and described the situation to Sally.

"Perhaps you could join me," I hesitantly suggested. Sally was a nurse. A decade before in the Transkei, South Africa, she had been my scrub nurse. I could use her supportive presence at my side.

"You haven't been in the OR for five years," she said, "and except for those six weeks in South Africa, I haven't been there for thirty. And ten years ago in South Africa, at least you'd brought all your equipment. No, with you free-wheeling this and me so long out of practice, what kind of team would we make? I think I can serve you and Manyoro better if I spend the time praying for his healing, as slim as that chance may be."

A few hours later, I watched the anesthesiologist prepare to place the mask over Manyoro's face. Then there was an abrupt pause. Had something gone wrong? I looked around and saw one of the nurses lean forward. In a barely audible whisper, she began praying for Manyoro. The tension lines in his face softened as she prayed. When she'd finished, the anesthesiologist gently placed the mask on Manyoro's face, and a few deep breaths later, he was ready for us to position him for surgery.

Well, *there* was something I'd never seen in an OR in the States.

I asked the staff again to keep looking for those additional units of blood we probably would need, and then, with my scalpel poised just over Manyoro's skin, I paused. I remembered those first operations in medical school so clearly now. There is something both magical and frightening about drawing that crimson line down the center of a human's body. It is the beginning of both an adventure and a challenge. It always got my blood running.

Moments later, as I grasped the hemostats (surgical clamps) and began coagulating the small blood vessels, a hint of assurance crept in. Maybe it *would* be like riding a bike after all.

And Lord, I can use all the help you can give me! I prayed silently.

Once I had cut through the skin, it was easy to find the problem. Manyoro's violent injury had torn the muscles away from the bones of his spine, and with simple retraction of his paraspinous muscles we could look right into the spinal canal. There was the cord, flat, its normal conical shape compressed by the dislocation. I placed the sucker over the blood clots that surrounded it, evacuating the hemorrhage and returning the crimson-colored dural protective membrane to its normal glistening white. I ran my fingers along the dura. The cord beneath this substantial covering appeared to be in continuity. No sense opening it; there was no way we could repair a neural disruption with our primitive surgical tools.

I freed up more of the tissue to facilitate realigning the stack of vertebrae which had been so violently ripped out of alignment. Among the various surgical specialties, we orthopedic surgeons are typically stereotyped as clumsy jocks, all brute strength and no finesse. I thought about that as I tried to wrestle Manyoro's vertebrae back into alignment. It *did* take all my strength to get them realigned, so maybe the typecasting was right after all.

But no sooner had I released the clamps than the bones sprang back to their deformed position. Creating stability was not going to be easy.

"This patient is lucky you got here when you did," the nurse anesthetist said. "To have a spine surgeon from the States—wow, he's really blessed."

"I wish it were that simple," I said. "What this guy needs isn't a spine surgeon from the States—he needs a miracle, and it's providential that my wife is praying for him all morning."

I looked over the orthopedic "junk" supplies on the back table to see what I might be able to use to hold the dislocated spine in place. The tibia plate was too big; the forearm plates were way too small. That left just a bunch of screws and some wires, nothing strong enough to hold a dislocated spine.

Then I remembered a research proposal I'd gotten a few years before while I was still president of Kirschner Medical. It was from one of our consulting surgeons—a request for funding. Teaming up with a surgeon from Finland, he had come up with a way to use screw fixation in a radically different way, beginning on the "wrong" side (meaning opposite the customary side) of the spinous process. The traditional means of screwing the two facet joints of each vertebra, as done in the 1950s, had long been abandoned because of the high failure rate of fusions with this technique. I had reoperated on a few cases done in this way by other surgeons, so I knew how ineffective it was. But this was something different. If a much longer screw was inserted from the *opposite* side and through the lamina bone, as the proposal that had come across my desk had suggested, it would traverse a stronger and much larger segment of bone, the entire bony shell that forms the covering over the spinal cord. And best of all, it would be at a right angle to the joint, creating optimal security.

The writer of the proposal I'd seen had wanted to test this new approach on animals using absorbable screws he and his co-researcher had just developed. His detailed proposal was intriguing, but I had elected not to approve it. At that point, Kirschner didn't have the resources for such a risky, unproven fusion technique. Still, intrigued, I had kept the proposal on my desk for a few weeks. It was truly a unique way to place the screws and certainly provided a more secure fixation.

But I'd never seen the procedure done. To my knowledge, it had been tested only on a few primates in the proposal writer's lab. As I considered the damage to Manyoro's spine, with the surgical team waiting around me for my decision, all I had to go on was the dimly remembered diagram in the proposal. I wasn't sure I remembered exactly how it was supposed to work. Even so, it might be Manyoro's only chance.

I made a small incision on the opposite side of the dislocation and tunneled through the overlying muscle. Drilling an oblique hole that would now parallel the bony spinal lamina, I placed the screw on the *wrong side* of the spinous process, manually closed the fracture-dislocation one more time, then had my novice surgeon-assistant turn the screw into its new position through the dislocation. We repeated the procedure coming from the opposite side. I'm sure that, without a diagram, the procedure is hard to visualize, but it was surprisingly easy to do. The question was, would it hold?

When I took my hands off . . . nothing happened! I waited for the fracture dislocation to spring back into its deformed place as it had each time I'd manually reduced it before.

It didn't move!

I couldn't believe it. But was it strong enough?

I grabbed a clamp and gently pulled on the previously dislocated vertebrae. They held rigidly together in the proper position.

With mounting excitement, I pulled a little harder—still no movement.

Perhaps overzealously, I pulled enough to lift Manyoro (still suitably anesthetized) a few inches off the operating table. The two vertebrae still did not separate.

I looked up and said to the nurse anesthetist, "The case is finished. I will be closing."

"But . . . we're barely twenty-five minutes into the case," she said in confusion. "I haven't even started the blood yet."

"Well, start to wake him up, because it isn't going to take me long to close," I said. I knew she couldn't see my smile behind my surgical mask, but I was sure she heard it in my voice. "And we won't be needing any blood—looks like he lost only a teaspoon or so!"

OK, OK—so I was exaggerating! I was relieved and excited. Placing the stitches in the damaged muscle, I realized that the bike I hadn't ridden for so long, surgery, was pedaling along just fine. The closing went quickly. Turning Manyoro over, I looked carefully for signs of recurrent deformity. There were none.

As I walked out of the OR, I picked up his chart to write the postoperative orders. I found a note by the hospital chaplain, written just a few minutes before he was taken into the OR, after my pre-op orders. It said, "I spoke with Manyoro about his paralysis and what he might expect in the future. I asked him if he knew Jesus. He said no. But after I explained to him the message of the gospel, he made a personal commitment of faith in Jesus Christ. We prayed together then that Jesus would heal him."

When I checked Manyoro later in the day, there was no difference in his neurologic status. He could still tell the position of his toes, but he couldn't feel them, and he certainly couldn't move them.

But he was very different in another way. His frightened, combative aggression from our first conversation had vanished. And each subsequent visit provoked a broader grin. A new Bible lay at his bedside. The nurses complained that Manyoro constantly wanted to talk to them about what he had recently read. "Do you know that Jesus loves you? He loves me too," was the way he would often begin those conversations. "Did you know that Jesus rose from the dead?" he would continue. "It was a miracle. Maybe I'll have a miracle. I asked Jesus for one. I ask him every day. What do you think?"

It was about five days later when Manyoro began to feel sensation in his left thigh. Was it just hope on his part, or was it real? The next day, he claimed to feel sensation in his lower right leg. We were beginning to see recovery.

Within three weeks he had feeling down to his toes and could flex his left knee. Each day brought further signs of recovery. And each day his faith grew. Six weeks after the surgery, Manyoro walked out of the hospital carrying his Bible, telling everyone that Jesus was God's Son and that he still performed miracles!

"And," he would always add, "he healed me too."

After the excitement of that first patient, Sally and I developed a routine. I'd get up at 5:00 a.m. and head off to the hospital to see the patients—all sixty-five of them. Then I would head home for a quick bite of breakfast around 6:30. I would return to harass the orderlies to get my first patient to the OR by 7:15, and I would make the incision by 7:30 on the first of five, six, occasionally seven operations. Then it was a short walk home, and I'd have late afternoon tea with Sally.

Sally's days were just as challenging, perhaps even more challenging. In contrast to my hectic schedule of too many patients, too little time, she spent long days actively but patiently seeking guidance from the Lord. *Our days with Kirschner are over,* she would pray. *We love the kind of short-term medical missions we've been involved in. Could it be, God, that you are asking us to leave our home, our children, our grandchildren to come to Africa?*

Africa—sure, why not? It made complete sense, given that we were now free to follow God's call on our lives. Why not start here? But it would be, to say the least, an immense change for us, so doing it for the wrong reasons would be disastrous. If we weren't doing it out of devotion and obedience to Christ, it was doomed to fail.

We foresaw two roles for me in this new life, if indeed we were going to launch into it. One was obvious: I would be doing exactly what I had been trained to do and had a passion for. I would have the joy of performing surgery on children who could barely walk—or couldn't walk at all—so that they could become productive citizens. The cases I loved best for the joy and satisfaction they brought to me, and for the hope and possibilities for a future the process brought to the patients, were those where the patient came into the hospital crawling on all fours. Two or three operations later, with a set of braces, maybe a cane, occasionally some crutches, they would walk out, able for the first time in their lives to look at their peers eyeball to eyeball. No words of reassurance could possibly create the same sense of self-worth. No sermon could as clearly communicate that those young patients were truly children of God, made in his image, and that he loved them.

But I also envisioned a second role for myself—an executive role. Why not take the skills and knowledge I'd acquired during my four years running an international orthopedic supplies company and apply it not just here in Kenya but also in the other two countries of British East Africa, Uganda and Tanzania, and perhaps even in Malawi, where I'd first worked ten years previously? Perhaps similar hospitals could be built in countries hostile to Christian missionaries but not to Christian doctors caring for their desperately needy disabled children in specialty hospitals focused on their needs. I envisioned, not just in Africa but worldwide, a network of hospitals for crippled children, somewhat like that created by the Shriners but with one big difference. In the hospitals I envisioned, there would be a significant emphasis on the spiritual needs of the patients and their families as well as on their medical needs. Starting and funding that network of hospitals, and administering it as CEO, would be my second role.

Those would be my roles—but what about Sally? This change, if it happened, would mean giving up her work at our church back in Pennsylvania. She had just begun a church-wide prayer ministry. The women's ministry that she had headed so diligently for several years was flourishing. She was actively involved in the mentoring and support of young women. All of that would end if we were to move to Africa.

We would be leaving our friends.

Short-term missions, the side of missions we had experienced in the past, are exhilarating times of drawing nearer to God. The possible future I envisioned wasn't part-time. It would be back-breaking work, it would take *all* of our time—and it might also consume our savings!

We loved the people of Africa. But were we committed to full-time work there? And was our vision for the network of hospitals God's leading—or was it just our own idea? We needed to hear the answers to those questions clearly from God.

I'd always been fascinated that three-quarters of Jesus's miracles involved healing. The physical change was an adumbration, a preview, of the even greater spiritual miracle of eternal life. It was his blueprint for spreading the good news.

As I watched Manyoro's healing progress, I wrestled more and more with the question: *Am I ready to seize this opportunity? Could I make a difference not only in one man's life but in the lives of thousands of children in this country ... and dozens of other countries besides?*

These questions monopolized our late-afternoon tea discussions. But not once did we argue about taking this big step: it was far too important and its implications for our lives too far-reaching for either of us to try to convince the other of our point of view.

Only through prayer would we be able to come to a decision that we could trust. For Sally, that meant day-long sessions of prayer—while overlooking the Rift Valley, taking in the splendor of God's handiwork, marveling as the light changed over the broad landscape with the extinct crater of Mt. Longonot rising in the distance. Continually seeking God's mind about this potential life change. Exhausting herself in prayer.

We'd been in Kijabe nearly five weeks when clarity came to Sally—not in a roar from the mountaintop but in that still small voice the Bible tells us to expect.

Go.

When I returned from the hospital that afternoon, Sally quietly said, "I'm confident that God's will for us is to begin this work. I have his assurance. God has answered my prayers … *our* prayers."

So it wasn't just Manyoro's prayers that the Lord had heard! Manyoro's prayers had been answered by God's provision for his injuries so that he could walk again. Sally's prayers, and mine, had been answered by God's invitation to us to walk as he leads.

When I asked God exactly how he intended for us to proceed, I was relieved when he answered, "*There are 140 million crippled kids in the world who need healing. Let's get started.*"

That was a much more welcome message than the one that had told me to get involved in business. From age ten, I had wanted to be an orthopedic surgeon so I could take care of crippled kids. In med school, I had chosen a research project that allowed me to work with the professor of orthopedics who had written one of the two textbooks on children's orthopedic problems. I had chosen my residency based on the opportunity it provided to study under the man who'd written the other. I'd chosen a location to begin my orthopedic practice that enabled me to work at the state "crippled children's hospital." I had spent my working life as a surgeon with children who had been disabled, so I had the medical skills to help them.

I knew from the start that this new effort, whatever it was to be called, would have to be international in scope. Most of the disabled children we hoped to serve didn't live in the United States or even in Western countries, parts of the globe that already had ample medical resources. We would have to go where the needs were. And there I had a bit of a start: Besides the medical missions work I'd been doing for several years, 46 percent of Kirschner Medical's sales had been international. So I already had a fair understanding of the differences between the international medical world and the medical situation in the United States.

Sally and I were excited—we wanted to get started immediately. The only problem: neither of us knew the slightest thing about nonprofits, and even less about starting an international ministry.

CHAPTER 6

CURE IS A REALITY!

"YOU DON'T WANT TO GET YOUR NONPROFIT OFF ON THE wrong foot by setting unrealistic goals," advised the consultant hired to help us conceptualize the new international medical organization Sally and I felt God leading us into. We had hired him at the suggestion of one of our board members. "Set obtainable goals," he continued. "That way you not only give yourselves a sense of accomplishment year by year as you achieve those goals, but you can also demonstrate to your donors and supporters that you're achieving the plan."

For our first meeting with him, we chose the lobby at the hotel Sally and I were staying in. Our consultant, an engaging person I immediately liked, had no health-care background. He also had no international business background. Still, he was a nice guy, well meaning, and trying to be helpful. I knew I needed to learn a lot, and quickly. I didn't argue with him, but the truth is, his idea didn't sit well. If we were really relying on prayer, on the Lord's partnership, shouldn't Christ be determining our future, and shouldn't our opinion of whether our goals were "obtainable" be determined by our faith in his ability to accomplish his will?

"So," the consultant continued, "what kind of goals did you have in mind?"

"I want to open one new hospital a year," I said.

An ambitious goal? Certainly. Our consultant just shook his head. He doubted we could do it. I understood his skepticism—in fact, my own experience told me that, in human terms, it was unrealistic. Twenty years before, I had partnered with a friend in building for-profit rehab hospitals using venture-capital funding. My friend was a genius at obtaining financing—but even so, we failed to meet our goal of one new hospital a year. In that project, however, I hadn't been relying on prayer.

When it came to CURE, I believed that the power of prayer would get these hospitals built.

Our consultant suggested that if we *were* to reach that goal, we would need $100 million in the first ten years. That, as it turned out, was a low estimate—we would eventually need four times that. Part of that budget would be for hospital construction and part for operating costs. The hospitals we planned to build would be of several different types. We would need some that could internally generate funds (such as the Oasis Hospital we would eventually build in Al Ain, east of the capitol of Abu Dhabi in the United Arab Emirates) and some that would generate only a minimal amount of operational funds because they would be focused on serving the very young and tragically poor—such as the pediatric neurosurgical hospital we would later build in Mbale, Uganda.

My years at Kirschner had given us the resources to get started. But clearly we would need much more than Sally and I could contribute. Even worse, not only did I not have enough money, but I didn't think of myself as much of a fund-raiser either.

Honestly, I wasn't even sure God could raise the hundreds of millions of dollars we would need.

The more I concentrated on my own shortcomings, though, the more I realized that, in Scripture, many of those God called tried to weasel out of their God-given challenges by pointing out to him that he had the wrong candidate for the job.

Moses was a man with a great education and family connections, ready to start a promising career. One day he lost his temper and killed a man. He sneaked out of the country to avoid prosecution and, in a distant nation, worked an entry-level position as a shepherd. He married the boss's daughter, but by the time he was eighty (age seemed to mean different things in Old Testament times than it does today), he was in a dead-end situation.

Yet God recruited him for the job of negotiating—with the most powerful man in the world, the Pharaoh of Egypt—the release of two million slaves, who happened to be the backbone of the Egyptian economy.

The list of "reluctant heroes of faith" goes on: Gideon, whose clan was the weakest, was empowered to drive out the oppressor; David, only thirty years old, with no military or legislative experience, was called by God to defeat the Philistines by relying on God rather than on David's armies; Peter, a commercial fisherman with no preaching background, was called to be the foundation stone of the church built on Christ's ministry. We can all think of people who did more than they or others expected, and they did it through the strength of the Lord. As I looked at other scriptural examples of individuals whom God chose for important jobs, it became clear that although they were very different in many ways, there was something they had in common: They initially tried to avoid the call God had placed on their lives by insisting that they were incapable of doing it. They insisted that God had called the wrong person.

It's obvious, in retrospect, why God chose such people. It was to him that the glory was to come, not to these people whom we see as biblical heroes. So my excuses for why I couldn't found what is now called CURE International didn't hold up.

(And no, no, no, I don't put myself in the company of these heroes!)

⌒

Sally and I began to ask ourselves some hard questions. And the first was fundamental to the entire initiative: how should we combine the spiritual and medical ministries?

By then I'd worked in twenty-five to thirty hospitals in Africa. It was often hard to tell the mission hospitals from those run by the country's government, not because of the equipment and quality of care but because one was as likely—or, for that matter, as unlikely—to include a spiritual component as the other.

On one of my mission trips, I treated an elderly man who had been in a hospital for months. His right hip had broken and failed to heal. In the States, a metal hip replacement would have been implanted a few days after his fracture, and by now he would have been home playing with his grandchildren. But neither this hospital, nor his family, could afford even the few hundred dollars for a developing-world inexpensive copy of what is routinely used in the States.

So I suggested instead a hundred-year-old operation that, although leaving his leg slightly shorter, would allow him, in the few remaining years of his life, to walk pain-free. I'm not sure what the staff said as they relayed that information to him, but he didn't seem relieved. Rather, he remained anxious right up to the moment when we put him on the operating table.

The anesthesiologist then asked, "So who will pray for this man?"

Our diminutive scrub nurse nodded and walked to the head of the OR table. Only our patient could hear her soft voice as she bent close and began to quietly pray. Finally he began to relax. A faint smile erased some of the wrinkles of his weathered face, and he was asleep before the medication was administered.

I could tell many similar stories. I believed, based on those experiences, that creating an intentional spiritual-medical combination ministry can be done—not by regulations, but by encouraging the development and expression of the faith of those who care for the patients. Experiences like this germinated into our fifty-fifty principle of equal medical-spiritual care.

On the day I operated on that elderly man, looking out the window as I waited for the anesthesiologist to give the go-ahead, it dawned on me: this was a regional government hospital, not a mission hospital. In the States, although he would have received his metal hip in just a few days, he would have done so without the balm of prayer. Here, even though we were in a government hospital, prayer was understood to be essential. Sadly, I've never seen prayer in a Stateside OR other than on the lips of the patient.

Despite experiences such as that one, prayer was still hit or miss. That patient received it—other patients even in mission hospitals sometimes did not. So as Sally and I considered alternatives, our dilemma was: How do we make sure the spiritual dimension of our work doesn't get lost? The medical side always seems to be more urgent, yet for Sally and me, the spiritual side was the driving force behind the whole project. How do we apportion the emphasis between medical and spiritual?

After much more discussion, we decided to aim for an even split: 50 percent of everything we did in our new organization would be spiritual ministry, and the remaining 50 percent would be the medical ministry. This meant that our facilities would have two equal leaders: the medical director and the spiritual director. That may not sound revolutionary, but in the male-dominated culture of Africa, it was unfathomable to have orthopedic doctors (most likely male) share equal status with a possibly female director of spiritual ministry. And it would be not just the medical directors who would have a hard time accepting this; the spiritual directors would find it just as difficult to accept.

At one hospital we hired Linda and Harold, husband and wife, as our spiritual ministry team. But her obvious leadership abilities prompted us to name her the spiritual director and her husband the assistant spiritual director. Even though, as a couple, they understood the wisdom of that, she insisted, when they left the hospital to do outreach in areas where there might be future patients, that Harold act as the senior leader. "Otherwise, none of them will come!" she said. "They'd have no respect for either of us."

When CURE became a reality, we even spelled out that if the spiritual director was making progress in introducing a patient to the gospel, they could write in the chart, "Do not discharge this patient." They had the same privileges as the surgeon, and used them.

If our fifty-fifty principle was the primary operational directive of the organization Sally and I wanted to create, a strong second was our determination that each hospital be a teaching hospital. No charitable organization, not even the Gates Foundation, has the resources to reach the world's 140 million curable disabled children. Part of our mission was to help train resident medical specialists to meet these needs within each country we served. Ultimately, long-term success in country after country around the world would come through a national cadre of trained indigenous specialists.

In one respect, this focus on teaching made our ambitions easier to fulfill. Smaller specialty teaching hospitals of typically thirty to a hundred beds require much less in capital costs than primary-care government institutions that often contain a thousand or more beds.

Finally we decided that we would hold our facilities to First World quality results. Fortunately, we could do so freed from the regulations (however well-intentioned) and the toxic legal environment that has created a prohibitively expensive cost structure in the First World. Functioning outside that framework, we could achieve similar quality for three to nine cents on the dollar. And that pattern extends to other areas of medical specialty, and to other areas of the world, as well. The cost in most of the world for open-heart surgery, performed to First World standards, is $6,700, whether you're in Sri Lanka, Argentina, Brazil, India, even Palestine—and it allows a fair profit. Open-heart surgery in America costs $70,000 to $200,000, with no better quality of care or outcome!

These were the principles behind the hospitals that were eventually to form the CURE International system. We started the ministry in 1995 when we began the reconstruction of a hundred-year-old mission hospital in Kijabe, Kenya.

Openings of new hospitals followed quickly:

- 1998 Kijabe, Kenya
- 2000 Mbale, Uganda
- 2002 Blantyre, Malawi
- 2003 Santo Domingo, Dominican Republic

- 2004 San Pedro Sula, Honduras
- 2006 Al Ain, United Arab Emirates
- 2006 Kabul, Afghanistan
- 2006 Lusaka, Zambia
- 2008 Addis Ababa, Ethiopia
- 2010 Niamey, Niger
- 2013 Davos, Philippines

There were also offshoots. In 2006 we formalized a program of outpatient clubfoot care that is now called CURE Clubfoot. It was in twenty-seven countries by 2013. In 2011, CURE Hydrocephalus was officially begun.

Frustratingly, when I stepped down after sixteen years, we had been unable to create hospitals in many other countries where serious needs existed.

↩

As we began the ministry and the ground for those first few hospitals was being broken, hanging over my head was more than just the cost of those first efforts—I was also concerned about the annual operating costs of this breakneck pace of hospital openings. But I felt we had to keep up that pace to meet the desperate needs of disabled children around the world. My projections showed that we would need not just millions of dollars, nor even tens of millions, but ultimately more than a hundred million.

A partial answer to that problem had been given to me years earlier by a speaker who came to the Methodist church I grew up in. He was the industrialist R. G. Letourneau. I was fascinated more by how he had lived than by what he said. He had tithed a tenth of his income for his entire life until he became financially successful, at which point he switched to what he described as an "inverted tithe." He kept 10 percent for himself and gave the Lord 90 percent.

That idea stuck with me more vividly than any preaching or Scripture that I've heard for years before or since. I can still remember, in fact, where I was sitting in the sanctuary that night, looking up (literally and figuratively) at this man. I saw in him a joy, an excitement, and an indefinable radiance. At the time, I understood this only at a superficial level: his sacrifice and obedience and identification with Christ brought him joy. Even though I didn't fully comprehend it, it whispered to me over the years.

Now I was to experience it more fully.

At the time we started CURE International, I was a tither. Most of that money had been going to our local church and some to other Christian ministries. But that first year of CURE, in order to have the funds to create our first hospital, Sally and I octupled our giving.

Gradually, over the next few years, we increased that level again and again, until we were giving twelve times the original amount. That funded our failed second hospital project in Tanzania as well as our Uganda neurosurgical hospital.

Naturally I wondered what this level of giving, especially if we were to maintain it long-term, meant—not just to CURE International and our ability to construct hospitals, but also, potentially, to our personal retirement savings. We were, after all, at this point giving more to CURE than we were earning. And it is a strange feeling to realize that you have given away your entire yearly income, and then some.

But there was another way to look at it: The Lord was transforming the success I had had in business into far greater successes. He was taking money that was simply gathering interest and using it to gather souls for the kingdom. That truth was impossible to resist. As the number of healed crippled children kept growing, so did our giving! And our joy continued to grow in seeing the expressions of grief on the faces of afflicted children and their families transformed into smiles by the love of God.

And what a joy the first time CURE got the chance to bring healing to countries that *excluded* Christian organizations. When the president of Afghanistan offered to give a rebuilt hospital to the openly Christian CURE rather than to an Islamic nonprofit (see chapter 7), it was an opportunity we couldn't refuse. We would just have to find the funds. For Sally and me, that meant doubling our financial support to twice our annual income. But it was an investment that has paid dividends many times over: now CURE is the largest Christian presence in this 99 percent Muslim country.

Of those we tried and failed at, North Korea was the lost opportunity I most regret. After a week of nonstop negotiation in Pyongyang, we had a signed agreement with the Ministry of Disabilities. Shortly after that, President Kim Jong-il died. Now, as long as his son continues exploding nuclear bombs in violation of agreements his father had signed, there is no chance of resurrecting that project. Many expatriate Koreans are praying that it will ultimately be built. We hope you'll add your prayers to theirs.

To meet these unique opportunities in closed countries, Sally's and my giving continued to increase. Am I bragging? Am I humbled to have the chance to give? Actually, neither is true. I did this because I'm selfish. I have been given an opportunity to work closely with the Lord of the universe. My part is infinitesimally small, but at least I do have a part. We are changing lives. More correctly, *he* is changing lives. Paralyzed children walk. Parents tormented by demons of doubt and fear are made whole.

I would like to say that healing children is what motivated me, and it did—but that isn't the whole story.

I'm motivated by the ways in which God has changed me. I'm having a love affair with the greatest source of love imaginable. And as a by-product, I'm being transformed as well.

I recounted in chapter 4 how, years ago, I was hesitant to hand over control of my life to Jesus because I was afraid of what would happen. I thought life wouldn't be fun anymore. In a childlike way, what I feared most about giving control of my life to Christ was what he might ask of me. Might God force me to be a preacher, or never marry, or—God forbid!—might he even ask me to go to Africa! I couldn't be a doctor there, could I?

What I failed to understand was that the thing I feared most actually constituted an offer from God for the opportunity of a lifetime: a life of joy and fullness and closeness to the Lord.

During my years with CURE, I've witnessed 140,000 children changed by reconstructive surgery that corrected their disabilities. Even better, I've seen nearly the same number of people make confessions of faith, begin to regularly attend church, and spread the good news of what they experienced to hundreds of thousands of friends, family members, and even a few enemies.

CHAPTER 7

A CLINIC
IN AFGHANISTAN

IT WAS DECEMBER 2001, JUST THREE MONTHS AFTER THE
World Trade Center attack, and the United States had recently
gone to war in Afghanistan. I attended an Advent service at
which the pastor, not surprisingly, was talking about the three
wise men. He mentioned that some scholars believe they may
have come from southern Afghanistan.

Because I had spent a fair amount of time in the Middle East,
that statement reminded me of something: Shame and honor are
now, as they have been dating back to antiquity, the essence of
Middle Eastern culture. To those unfamiliar with their culture,
Middle Easterners may seem to be extravagantly nice. Dinners
are more elaborate than expected. Concern for your health and
that of your family is expressed upon each new meeting. They
honor you in many ways, some you aren't even aware of.

But there is a flip side to that principle of honor—a darker
side. If the recipients of these generous gestures are unable to
reciprocate, they are dishonored. Until the debt is repaid—until
they are able to pay their host back in an amount equal to or even
more extravagant, no matter the price—the original recipient is
shamed.

As my pastor continued his sermon about the three wise men, I wondered: Had that initial kindness of the wise men, unreciprocated, been perverted into shame for the recipient? Might the generous gifts of gold, frankincense, and myrrh by these magician rulers from southern Afghanistan left Joseph in dishonor because he could not, as a carpenter of modest means, respond appropriately? Strange as it seems to a Western mind, Joseph may have left for Egypt dishonored!

There is no doubt that, if that debt is viewed from the perspective of two thousand years of Christ's work in the lives of billions of people, it has been paid back and then some—but not directly to the generous wise men.

As that Advent service neared its end and we bowed in prayer, I found myself thinking, *I can repay these gifts from the wise men by bringing a CURE hospital to their descendants still living in Afghanistan.*

A little goofy? Sure, I admit it. But sitting in that church pew, I felt there was at least a germ of truth, if not actual inspiration, in the idea. By that time, CURE had built six or seven hospitals. Our strategy was to place hospitals, if possible, in areas where other Christian nonprofits could not go. Afghanistan fit that model perfectly.

A few months and a few dozen phone calls later, I was in the Pakistani city of Quetta—the unofficial capital, although I didn't know it at the time, of the Taliban terrorist group. Our hotel was, in fact, the backdrop for their television interviews. Fools walk in . . .

We met two young Southern Baptist missionaries who were masquerading as agricultural consultants. The day before we set out to drive the twelve hours to Kandahar in Afghanistan, one of them asked if I would visit a Hazara Shia Muslim couple with whom he'd been meeting. The husband, Jamiat, was a nurse; his wife, Alya, was an invalid who hadn't walked in six months despite her visits to a number of doctors, some as far away as Karachi, an eight-hour drive south. Not one of those doctors had come up with a diagnosis, much less a treatment plan.

The next morning, I climbed a steep stone stairway to their apartment. Entering a large room that served as both living room and dining area, I caught sight of Alya lying propped up in a nest of blankets in the back hallway. It would have been culturally unacceptable for me to see her in their marital bed, and the main room was already filling with friends and relatives gathered for this unusual visit from a Western doctor. Alya, anxious and uncomfortable with all the attention, pulled her veil around her face.

Jamiat, his brows pulled tight with worry, gave me a brief history. Alya was in her early twenties, the mother of three children she could no longer care for. There had been no injury, but her infirmity had developed quickly, and it had been six months since Alya had been able to do any housework or cook a meal. She was now unable to get out of bed.

My attempt at a physical exam, with her sprawled on the hallway floor, became a battle between my need for discovery and her need for modesty. Both legs were swollen and limp, showing moderate pitting edema. Her pale skin was feverish, her fingertips cyanotic (tinged with blue from inadequate oxygen).

In diagnosing medical conditions, sometimes you get lucky. My guess is that the telltale butterfly rash over Alya's nose, a distinctive characteristic of her illness and a question traditionally asked on every medical school quiz in internal medicine, hadn't been there when the doctors in Karachi had seen her. Or perhaps those examinations had taken place early enough in the development of her illness that the blood tests were not conclusive. Or maybe she had just seen bad doctors!

This beautiful woman's diagnosis was severe *Lupus erythematosus*, an autoimmune disease in which the patient's immune system attacks its own healthy tissue, destroying various organs. I'd rarely seen lupus so far advanced. Alya's kidneys were already failing, which explained the swelling in her legs. Her heart would be next. Normally, First World treatment would consist of expensive steroids and anticancer drugs, but Jamiat and Alya could never afford those. It looked as if there was nothing I could do for her.

Well, that wasn't entirely true—I could pray for her.

But would her husband allow a white Christian, American stranger to pray for his Muslim wife? I had just explained to him that the mother of his three children had an incurable disease and that her life expectancy was limited. His attitude toward me at the moment couldn't be very positive.

The noise from the adjacent room was becoming intrusive, since many more of Alya's Hazara neighbors had arrived. Quetta was a center for the fundamentalist Sunni Muslims of Pakistan, and the neighbors knew that an American doctor was in the hallway. To them, *American* meant *Christian*. I had no way to decipher the increasing buzz of conversation, but I was pretty sure it was about me. It was unusual enough that this Christian had examined a devout Muslim woman. Now it turned out that I couldn't help her in her illness. Tense hardly characterizes the moment.

Even so, I asked Jamiat if I might pray for his wife. With a fatalistic nod, he agreed.

I began by confessing to the Lord that I was helpless. (The understatement of the morning!) I added that I was also concerned—well, let's be honest, I was frightened—about what might happen if one of those devout fundamentalist Muslims, perhaps a terrorist, found out that a Christian was praying for Alya.

I confessed that the woman for whose comfort or perhaps even healing I was praying did not know his Son. But in the past, I reminded him, he had healed those who did not know him. And as if God didn't already know, I outlined the diagnosis and Alya's medical problems: fever, anemia, swollen ankles, early renal failure, photosensitivity, extreme fatigue, and so on, ending with her distinctive telltale butterfly rash.

I became as desperate in my pleas as the young husband.

I mentioned, as tactfully as I could to the God of the universe, that this might be an appropriate time for us to rebalance the shame and honor that had existed for two thousand years between the descendants of Joseph and Mary and those pagan wise men from the east, who might well have come from this area.

During my frantic prayer, even though I knew it might be culturally unacceptable, I laid my hands in desperation on Alya, not sure that I wouldn't feel the point of a butcher knife at my throat as a result.

Then it was over. I stood. I nodded to the woman and her husband, relieved that I hadn't so offended Jamiat that violence had ensued. Walking back into the living area, I saw that the crowd had enlarged to twenty-five to thirty uncles, cousins, and other kinfolk. I suggested to my young missionary friend that we leave before the husband described to the assembled multitude what had just happened.

Next morning, we began our twelve-hour ride to the ancient city of Kandahar, founded by Alexander the Great in the fourth century BC and now home to al-Qaeda. During the journey, we were blinded by one of the sandstorms endemic to this part of Pakistan that seemed symbolic of my Afghan visit so far. Then a seemingly endless series of switchbacks challenged our nerves as we climbed the mountains ever farther into the Taliban-controlled mountains. Occasionally we glimpsed the twisted wreckage of a truck a thousand feet below, reminding us of the unlucky drivers who had failed on one of these hairpin turns. On the way up, this was enough to make me uneasy but not terrified. That changed on the way down, when I realized that we would face certain death if we failed to navigate a turn—due to failing brakes, for instance. After all, in this part of the world, no friendly ambulance would come to rescue us.

Then we were back in the desert and, finally, at the border. It wasn't very busy that day. Actually, we were the only vehicle attempting to get into Afghanistan. It seemed that the war was discouraging tourism.

The border guards, intimidating with AK-47 rifles hanging from their shoulders, took our passports and insisted that we leave the car and go inside a stone house. That seemed better than staying out in the 100-degree sun, and besides, I didn't want to let my passport out of my sight since it was probably worth a few thousand dollars on the black market.

We were led into a living room large enough for fifty or so guests. A well-dressed man beckoned us from the far end. He arose from his overstuffed chair and waved his hand toward a group of similarly stuffed, embroidered chairs. He nodded to another armed attendant, who returned with a tray carrying cups, cookies, and a pot of tea.

Our host spoke surprisingly good English and seemed fascinated to have American guests. I mentioned that our goal was to build a hospital for disabled children in Afghanistan. Our host seemed puzzled as to why we would do such a thing.

An hour or so later, the waiter who'd brought us tea returned, now carrying his SKS-45, a bigger version of the border guard's rifle. He also returned my passport. With broad smiles and mutually unintelligible thanks, we got on our way.

Within a few miles, we came to the first of a series of blown-up bridges. In this parched landscape, they were needed only during the rainy season. A well-delineated road through the desert around the rubble made these obstructions only minor inconveniences.

A surprising number of these concrete bridges also served as hiding places for tanks. That didn't seem to have been an effective strategy, since we kept seeing gutted tanks sporting concrete hats. That room in Quetta with the thirty uncles and cousins seemed relatively safe now!

Kandahar is the second-largest city in Afghanistan. The historic center for the Pashtuns, it had become the epicenter of Taliban influence, but at the time of our visit, the American forces were in control—or so we had been assured. Despite our multiple trips to the US State Department and our meetings with religious groups working in that region, I still felt out of my depth.

I was anxious to see the proposed site for our hospital, so early the next morning we accompanied local officials to the western edge of town, where they pointed to a large sandy field. It had been six months since that Advent service at church, and in that six months I had been growing more and more eager to break ground. So as soon as the car stopped, my enthusiasm propelled me quickly to the center of the lot. I looked around, thinking, *This is perfect*. I also noticed that I was the only one out there. Where were the others? I looked back—the rest of the group still stood at the edge of the field, waving and yelling.

"Only this corner over here has been cleared of mines!" one local official shouted. "But just retrace your steps on your own footprints in the sand—you'll be fine!"

Sure I would. After all, I already knew there were no mines there—or else I would already have been blown up! I had galloped out into the field. Returning, I went very slowly, scrutinizing the ground to correctly identify each footprint. But since I had made them while running, they were farther apart than a normal walking stride. I was able to keep my balance most of the time as I lurched from footprint to footprint. And when my balance wavered, only luck, or my prayers, ensured that I didn't become suddenly airborne.

The corner of the field that had already been cleared of mines sported a tent to shield us from the blistering sun and a stone pillar with a bronze plaque commemorating the groundbreaking the following day of this new disabled children's hospital.

A few hours later, I met the local governor. His story was unforgettable: His father had preceded him as the warlord of this area of a couple of million people. As near as I could tell, his "election" as governor meant that he had a militia bigger than anyone else's. It also meant that he controlled one of the largest *cannabis indica* growing areas in the world. He was the personification of a drug lord! During the civil war that began after Russia had been expelled from Afghanistan in 1989, his father had been killed by another warlord. My host, I was told, eventually found the culprit, brought him to the town square, and lynched him. Then he sat under the swinging corpse until midnight, an AK-47 on his lap. By preventing the assassin's body from being buried before sundown, a requirement among Muslims, he inflicted the final ultimate shame on his adversary.

The next day, sitting beside him during the groundbreaking ceremony, I had difficulty getting that picture out of my mind. My new ally may have wondered why I was looking at him instead of the ceremony; I couldn't take my eyes off his bull neck. Would it even be possible to hang him? One of his many children, about six years old, sat beside me, as innocent and adorable as his father was frightening. We smiled a lot and shook hands a lot; we each gave a short incomprehensible speech; then we nodded at each other—the universal language. We concluded with anemic smiles.

After the interviews with CNN and the BBC, along with some toasts and tiny pastries, we headed over to meet the regional minister of health at the only hospital for the three million people in this area of Afghanistan. It was referred to as the "Chinese" hospital because it had been built thirty or so years before by China. I doubted that any medical representatives of that country had been back since—this facility made African hospitals look like modern medical centers by comparison.

It also looked like Times Square on New Year's Eve. The parking lot was jammed, not with cars but with people. Shouldering our way up the three floors to the minister's office took a half hour. But these crowds were not visiting the patients—they *were* the patients. There was no outpatient facility for medical care, so the halls of the hospital served as the outpatient clinic.

The minister thanked me for coming to build a hospital for disabled children. After another obligatory cup of tea, we muscled our way to the pediatric floor. Surrounded by the chaos that I was quickly learning was normal, half a dozen doctors were trying to see between eighty and a hundred children ranging in age from newborn to early teens. The docs shouted back and forth, trying to locate the one stethoscope they were all sharing. No X-rays. No lab. And no privacy! I'm sure that was tough on the adolescent girls, who would soon be wearing burkas.

The noise was stupefying. Babies wailing, toddlers screaming, parents shouting "I'm next!" in several different dialects. I got the idea! There was room for improvement here. We headed back to the minister's office for further discussion.

After rejecting an offer of more tea and hoping I hadn't committed an unpardonable breach of etiquette by doing so, I asked if we might talk further about the proposed children's disability hospital.

"First let me tell you about our proposed medical center!" he exclaimed. "Here is the master plan." He rolled out a large diagram, an overhead plan view. "You could put your hospital right beside the main building!" By now he was bouncing from foot to foot.

Was this the old bait-and-switch technique? He had already offered us a different parcel of land. Was his true intention to influence us into funding his dream of a medical center? I stood to study the diagram, then sat again slowly, thoughtfully. "This is an enormous undertaking for a country emerging from such a devastating civil war," I said. "And most of the destruction happened before America got involved. There are similar plans for Kabul and western Afghanistan, aren't there?"

"Yes, but I think your government will build this one also," he said, like a child anticipating what is under his Christmas tree. I elected not to point out that it was highly unlikely Uncle Sam would be creating and funding a hospital complex in the center of an area controlled by the Taliban.

"But you desperately need primary health care now," I said

instead, then began thinking out loud. "Perhaps we should reconsider the sequence of events. Didn't we pass a big, bombed-out building on our drive over here, about the size of half a city block? It appeared to be just a shell, but its walls looked solid."

"Yes, that's an old British administration building. It was gutted a long time ago. But you're correct—it was built like a fort. Maybe that's because we gave them such a beating at the end of the nineteenth century!"

"Might we be given this building? To build not a hospital, but a large multi-specialty clinic? It seems as if that's your most pressing need, based on what we just saw in the hallway on the pediatric floor." I could hear the excitement building in my voice. Why wait for a Western-built medical center that might never materialize when CURE could be helping Afghani children and adults within a few months?

For the next few days, we shuttled between various governmental departments. Again and again, the officials we spoke to pressed us to be part of the future medical center. And with each meeting, I became more and more insistent that, if the government would just make that old building available to us to renovate, they could quickly have appropriate health care of the type they most desperately needed. Lives would be saved. What could be more urgent?

Finally, after I half promised that *if* the proposed medical center ever got off the ground, we would consider building the children's hospital there, they made the former British administration building available for a clinic. They were happy to get this eyesore off their hands.

A few hundred thousand dollars and five hectic months later, we began seeing patients.

We immediately ran into our first major medical problem:

the Afghani doctors. They would sign in at 7:00 a.m. After a cup of tea, they would—despite the fact that they were receiving a stipend from the Afghan government to work as doctors—leave to see if they could find work driving a cab or repairing bombed-out buildings; more likely, they spent the day sipping tea and smoking. At 4:45 they would reappear, sign out at 5:00, and repeat the process the next day.

"We can't support our families on what the government is paying us," they explained—and this, at least, was true. What they didn't say was that, apparently, they didn't think international aid agencies such as CURE cared whether they worked or not—even though we had a clinic full of patients who needed care. So CURE negotiated with the doctors a sum adequate for survival in the Afghan postwar economy, and to reach that level of pay, CURE agreed to supplement the subsistence-level wage the government paid so that our doctors and their families wouldn't starve.

On the first day of our new arrangement, the docs signed in promptly at 7:00 a.m. Then, just as before, after a cup of tea, the majority took off to look for work in town. At 4:45, they reappeared. They signed out at 5:00. In other words, no change.

We explained that this was no longer acceptable.

Even after that, for most of them—no change.

We explained again. They nodded their heads, but again, no change—until the next pay period, when there were some surprises. The few doctors who had spent the entire day caring for patients got their pay raise, while those who had headed out to town and tea got their government check only.

They were irate. They had grown to expect that they could take advantage of every foreign not-for-profit operating in Kandahar. But there was more to come: We told them that if they didn't accept our wage system—increased pay for doing a *full day's work*—they would be fired. This, in their experience, was outrageous. Relief organizations didn't act like that. CURE was, I explained, a Christian humanitarian medical organization, not the UN. An honest day's work for an honest day's pay was our expectation and our rule.

Some of our would-be medical staff scoffed—they didn't believe we would hold them to it. They are driving cabs now.

Those who stayed, though, were eager for training. Since routine medical equipment hadn't been available for years, they had to learn, or relearn, basic medicine. But they were bright and hard working. Within a short time, the clinic was seeing 17,000 to 18,000 patients each month, one of whom was President Hamid Karzai. He was pleased when we asked him to pay $3.00 for his medicine. "A good example to the people," he said, loud enough for the TV cameras to catch. Then he quietly directed his assistant to pay.

Four years and 850,000 patient visits later, we transferred ownership and supervision of the clinic to the Regional Medical Department. They still haven't broken ground on their medical center complex, but the clinic continues providing care.

﹏

Remember Alya, the young woman with lupus whom I'd prayed for in Quetta? After we arrived in Kandahar, the missionary who had taken me to visit her phoned his companion, who had escorted us to Kandahar. He couldn't wait to tell me what had happened.

After we left, Jamiat had carried his wife back to bed and was gone for the rest of the day. When he returned, he immediately noticed the fragrance of cooking food. There in the kitchen was Alya. She had taken a nap after we left, and when she awoke, she had gotten out of bed, walked into the kitchen, and for the first time in six months, cooked dinner.

As day followed day, she continued walking, and the swelling in her legs gradually decreased. She began caring for her children, even washing the clothes. After a few days, it was clear that she could and would continue her normal duties as a mother and wife.

Three months later, two Islamic religious leaders came to "the house of the lady where Dr. Scott had prayed," as it had come to be known. They had heard the rumor of the healing that had taken place on July 23. With them was a mullah who was the official historian for this Hazara Islamic sect. He was to determine what had really happened.

His official report, which was spread throughout the Hazara community, was translated by my Baptist missionary friends:

> A busy American Christian doctor came to see Alya. She had been unable to walk for 6 months. He examined her and confirmed that she could not walk. It is to be recorded in the history of our people that after this American Christian doctor prayed to Jesus for Alya, a miracle happened! Alya was healed and now walks. She is cooking and doing all things she used to be able to do. She remains healed. It is to be recorded as a miracle. We are thankful and give all praise to Allah.
>
> Signed
> Mullah _____?

(His handwriting was as bad as a doctor's—I couldn't make out his name!)

CHAPTER 8

CURE—
WALKING THE WALK

WHEN WE WERE SEARCHING FOR A PLACE TO BUILD OUR
children's hospital in Kabul, Afghanistan, I would frequently
drive past the national soccer stadium. The stadium wasn't
impressive—really only the size of a typical high school football field in the States. As we drove past, my host told me of
the weekly public executions that the Taliban, when they ruled
the country, forced the citizens to attend. Islamic law, at least
as interpreted by these zealots, was a harsh, extreme version of
justice, based on passages of the Koran. Our guide pointed to the
area, for instance, where each Saturday morning, with accompanying shouts of "Allah is great," the Taliban cut off the right hand
of those caught stealing. At the end of the morning, the children
who lived in the city dump collected these hands, hoping some
might have a gold ring still attached. These practices associated
with Sharia law were discontinued by subsequent Muslim gov-
ernments after the United States military's defeat of the Taliban—
at the cost of 2,326 US soldiers killed and over 20,000 wounded.

The Taliban are not typical of the Muslims I've met in other
countries. Nevertheless, they remain a stealth force in Afghanistan even since being removed from power. Sadly, on the day I'm

writing this, March 20, 2016, fifteen government soldiers were killed by Taliban near Kandahar, not far from where we began our work. And as an unapologetic Christian, I was and remain the Taliban's enemy whom they are committed to destroy!

As I recounted in the previous chapters, we went on to build, in Kabul, our second Afghan hospital. More than any of our other hospitals, this was the one I felt most strongly led to complete. What turmoil Afghanistan had experienced in the decades before! An invasion by Russia, followed by a guerrilla war to oust the Russians, followed by a more destructive civil war; then finally another foreign power, the United States, ousting the Taliban minority who believed it was OK, even an expression of their devotion, to kill Christians, especially Americans.

Not all Americans, of course, are Christians. But CURE is unapologetically a provider of spiritual—meaning Christian—and medical healing. Those who have a different faith and do not believe they need such spiritual healing are still welcome to receive the same medical care at CURE hospitals as anyone else. We understand that they have a different understanding of God than we do, and we are sensitive to their beliefs, hoping that they will reciprocate. The overwhelming majority do.

A secondary precept of CURE is to train nationals to become health-care providers so they can ultimately provide the First World quality care that is desired by their countrymen. When CURE performs that service in a country of a different religious faith, especially one that is particularly hostile to Americans, how well will it be received—and how safe will CURE personnel in that country be? Those questions are never far from our minds when working under those circumstances—particularly in a country like Afghanistan.

Might a gentle answer turn away their wrath, as the biblical proverb suggests?

Perhaps. But optimism can't be an excuse for an irresponsible lack of safeguards. We believed, and events seemed to support our belief, that providing humanitarian health care without expectation of payment was a service important enough and valued enough by the host nation that it in itself provided a level of safety. The testimony among their own people by the Afghans who worked with us also helped.

All of us who came from the West to work in CURE's Kabul hospital were believers in Jesus Christ, and each of us in our own way felt called to this rugged, tragic country. We believed ourselves to be under God's protection, although we also realized that we could not presume it to be absolute, for many missionaries have been killed in the course of fulfilling their mission. So when a group of our staff, while hiking, was shot at by a young Afghani, we saw his wayward bullet as a sign of God's Providence.

Our fears concerning safety were not groundless. Dan Terry, who had assisted the hospital in many ways, was fatally shot at a terrorist checkpoint on August 5, 2010, in Badakhshan Province. Among the nine others killed in that incident was Tom Little, an optometrist working with the International Assistance Mission, or "I Am," who had built an eye hospital in Afghanistan. The reason the murderers gave for this slaughter: "They were talking about Jesus." The only survivor was an Afghani who could recite verses from the Koran!

As the bombings and killings continued around the CURE International Hospital in Kabul, the security walls grew higher—and CURE continued its efforts to gradually extract American personnel, replacing them with the Afghani doctors they had trained.

Initially, our security guards had been armed with pistols, holstered discreetly out of sight; as the situation worsened, we transitioned to men with rifles, very much in view. Then the walls were raised. Then they were raised again, and again, until they reached ten feet. Prominently displayed surveillance cameras added to the aura of security. Finally a cadre of soldiers from the Afghan National Security Guards was added for maximum safety.

In terms of security, in Kabul the gold standard was the United States Embassy. Taking up a full city block, its security walls were fifteen feet of reinforced concrete buttressed with sandbags to absorb the impact of potential car bombs. US military sentries with automatic rifles were placed every hundred paces. In comparison, we were pathetically underprepared. But then, I assumed that we didn't have as many enemies as they had.

One particular morning, like every other workday, Dr. Jerry Umanos approached our walled fortress on his way to starting his daily rounds. To the west, the morning sun highlighted the crumbled walls of the Darul Aman Palace, a relic of the violence of the internecine fighting among the mujahideen after the expulsion of the Russians. Jerry shook his head at this reminder of the violence endemic in this country. When he'd arrived nine years before, Kabul had been littered with crumbling buildings, their facades blown off, with refugees who had no alternative still living in them. And in the distance, snow still capped the mountains surrounding the city. *It is,* he thought, *in spite of everything, a beautiful place, and we've come a long way from those violent days.*

A member of the Afghan Security Force nodded as he signed in. He paused in the courtyard leading to the front door. The building now had a proper entrance rather than the utilitarian one it had had when he'd started working at the hospital.

What a difference, he thought. *No more bombs waking you in the middle of a dark night.*

He smiled as he entered his pediatric ward with its thirty-two children. These were his kids, at least while he sorted out their medical problems. How things had changed. Now the preemies survived. How well he remembered that tiny two-pounder who had clung so precariously to life. With the help of Vic, the other full-time American doc, they had constructed a makeshift incubator that had pulled him through. Now that child was playing soccer with his brothers.

Jerry's pediatric residents had the charts ready. The morning teaching rounds began. How many residents had he trained over the years?

"What's the biggest threat to this malaria patient?" he asked the new intern.

"What's the lowest level of hemoglobin that demands a transfusion?" he asked the senior resident, who answered quickly and correctly.

Jerry thoroughly enjoyed mentoring his residents in this way. And it produced excellent pediatricians. Probably more than fifty of them over the years? Sixty? Seventy? A lot, anyway. The best of them had joined the staff. The others were now bringing their First World quality medical care to other cities, occasional referring especially difficult cases to this hospital, to Professor Jerry.

A young mother, head modestly covered, smiled as she held up her baby. With the treatment Jerry and his team had provided, the baby's yellow skin had faded to a light auburn, the subdued color typical of his tribal area. He was ready to go home.

Speaking of home, Jerry remembered that a couple of friends from his home state were coming by today and should be here soon. He missed Chicago and his practice at the Lawndale

Christian Health Center. But as poor as that section of Chicago was, it was like paradise compared to where most of these children came from. There, he had been one of four hundred doctors who cared for nearly 190,000 patient visits a year. As most of their patients were indigent, it was important work. But here in Kabul they were worse off—destitute and so much sicker.

He looked at his watch, then nodded to his staff. "My guests should be at the entrance," he said, pocketing his stethoscope. Outside, he crossed the courtyard between the hospital and the entrance gate. His friends, Gary and his son, John Gabel, were waiting. John's wife, Teresa, was chatting with a nurse just coming off duty.

The nurse signed in first and headed to the entrance. John and his father waited as Jerry signed for them, then he gestured them inside ahead of him.

As the three men entered the courtyard, suddenly, without warning, lives changed—or ended—in a split second. The deafening roar of a Kalashnikov AK-47 screamed at them as it sent a torrent of 30-caliber bullets at 2,400 feet per second just an arms-length distance into the three men. They crumpled to the stone walkway.

Their killer, Aymuddin, barely paused. He had seen the American woman with the men just a moment before. He looked toward the hospital entrance—and there she was, desperately trying to reach the safety of the hospital. His cascade of bullets ripped through her belly. She crumpled just short of the door, falling awkwardly into the pool of her own blood that began to form around her.

He turned and looked directly into the security camera, a smile forming on his lips. Slowly he reversed the rifle, placing the barrel, now scalding hot, firmly against his chest, and squeezed the trigger. His hands reflexively opened, his rifle clattering onto the pavement. But it would be enough, he thought as he fell. It had found his vital spot. He would be dead in a few minutes. He had killed three infidels, he had earned his reward in the afterlife, and ninety-nine virgins awaited him in Jannah!

But wait—what was happening? It had been only a few seconds since his first bullet had extinguished that first hated American doctor's life. Now, the guards' strong hands grasped him, but not to strangle him. They weren't even beating him ... they were putting him on a stretcher. This isn't what he had planned. *Why have they not emptied their magazines of bullets into me? Where are they taking me?* He tried to get up, but the pain was too severe. When he opened his mouth to speak, blood gushed onto the man carrying him. He looked around him—and realized that he was being taken into the hospital. *Why? I just killed their doctor. I killed his two bastard American friends! Why aren't they killing me?*

Instead, the men carrying him raced down the hallway, shouting orders. He heard someone say, "Get two units of O negative blood!"

The lights in the OR blinded him. Someone stuck a needle in his arm. He became groggy ... then nothing.

⏎

Beside the entrance gate, Jerry and his two friends lay silently, motionless, surrounded by bullet casings floating in their blood. Jerry's blank eyes stared toward heaven. It was too late to do anything for the three of them.

But inside, it was the organized chaos of a well-trained surgical team. The injured nurse had been taken into another OR.

She too was in shock. With blood transfusions pouring into both of her arms, prayer and expert surgery began to turn the tide. "More blood—two more units!" was the cry of the surgeon as he placed clamp after clamp after clamp into the pool of blood that filled her abdomen, desperately trying to find the main bleeder that was inexorably taking her life.

Groping blindly, he felt the "hiss" of the lacerated renal artery between his thumb and index finger. He pinched it as you would a grape. Slowly, cautiously, he placed the hemostat just beside his fingers, close to where the renal artery was severed, clamping this main bleeder and insuring her survival. The suction gradually emptied the pooled blood. Without realizing, the surgeon had stopped breathing—not until he could see no further blood filling her abdomen did he exhale. Her recovery was no sure thing, but at least it was now probable. He paused ... probable? *No*, he thought, *with the training I've gotten from Dr. Vic, Jerry's friend, I know she will live!*

Aymuddin, if he had been conscious, would have been horrified. His surgery, performed by surgeons trained by Vic, was also going smoothly. The skin wound was extended proximally and distally. Hemostasis was achieved. The bullet had passed from the chest cavity through the diaphragm into the abdomen, so all twenty-six feet of the bowel was "run" to ensure that there were no unseen lacerations. The exit wound was kept open with a small drain to prevent an abscess. The few remaining bleeders were coagulated and the incision partially closed, because this high-velocity injury would result in necrosis of tissue that looked perfectly normal at the time of this initial surgery. The wound would be revisited in forty-eight hours, when Aymuddin might need some further excision of dead tissue.

As the medical team peeled off their masks, their expressions were conflicted—sorrow for their colleagues who were dead or injured, but satisfaction that this surgery had gone so well. The assassin would now live to face justice—or, more likely, receive a hero's adulation back in his village.

A few hours later, when Aymuddin regained consciousness, he was at first confused—this wasn't Jannah, the garden of perpetual bliss. Where were the magnificent gates by which he was to enter paradise?

And where were his virgins?

The truth sank in: He was still alive! How could this be? He had shot himself right through the heart! How could he have missed from an inch away? But there was no denying it—he was in the Christian hospital, and he was alive. The hated Christians had saved his life.

When the doctor told him that they had given him blood during the surgery, he was even more horrified: *It might have been Christian blood that saved my life!*

In anguish, he thought, *Not only have I failed to become a martyr, I may be tainted forever by these Christians who have saved my life. Are we now blood brothers? Might I even be like them ... a Christian?*

Aymuddin was stable the following day, so over the objections of our doctors at the CURE hospital, he was transferred to a government hospital.

There he might have become a hero to some, glorified for killing the infidels.

But to many Muslims, he is a cowardly assassin who killed unarmed healers who had come a long way and dedicated their lives to serving the people of Afghanistan who could not afford to repay them. They were repaid instead with an assassin's bullet —that is not how most Muslims understand the Koran! And then his countrymen, those who had been taught by the infidels, saved his life with their blood and their surgical skills!

Might having his life saved at a "Christian hospital" change him? What effect would the Christian blood flowing through his veins now have? It saved his life—but would his life also be transformed because it is "stained" by the Christian witness of unconditional love?

⤺

The story of the deaths of Jerry and his friends and the subsequent saving of the life of Aymuddin the assassin—and no, we don't know what happened to him after he left our hospital; it would put people at risk if they told us—is a powerful and meaningful story. But for me, this story has meaning far beyond the narrative I've related so far. This event, this story in all of its glory and tragedy, answered the greater question I asked when I began CURE sixteen years before: Could a Christian witness, wedded to medical care, impact those of other faiths, especially Islam? Could Jesus's message of loving even our enemies penetrate the cultural mores of an Islamic culture that historically had resisted Western influence in the most violent way?

After all, what greater love could we show than to save the life of an assassin who had, in hate, in cold premeditation, killed a man who had saved the lives of hundreds of the nation's children? By continuing to work in what was clearly a dangerously hostile country, Jerry had first risked his life and then met the greatest challenge given to Christians: He laid down his life for those God had enabled him to love.

I had hoped, sixteen years before, that CURE would emulate the example of Jesus.

Jerry had done just that.

PART 3

A Lifetime
of Surgery

CHAPTER 9

VIETNAM

BEFORE CURE, BEFORE I BEGAN PRIVATE PRACTICE, BEFORE my days as a CEO, there was the *mistake*—or at least that's what it became known as in the media and in conversation. Others just called it the war in Vietnam. It resulted in the deaths of 58,000 American soldiers and many more Vietnamese, at least 1.25 million. The war ended with South Vietnam becoming Communistic but united. But it divided our country, polarizing those who saw it as a necessary fight against Communism and those who considered it one of America's worst foreign policy blunders.

Thirty-five years later, I would attempt to build a hospital there. I failed.

But my years in the Vietnam War made me a surgeon. The traits of a good surgeon can be generalized as (1) prudent caution and, paradoxically, (2) measured aggression! Vietnam provided me with both.

In 1963, when I graduated from med school, almost all med students went into the services, either immediately after graduation or after their deferment for their residency ended. Why did we enlist? Because word was that, if you were drafted, you'd be made an orderly scrubbing floors. Whether that was true or not, the prospect scared most of us into volunteering. I picked up my med school diploma, went into an adjacent room, and raised my right hand to guard and protect the United States of America. Two years later, I was starting my final year of obligatory military service. It was a time of aggressive US military policy in Vietnam: President Johnson had begun sustained bombing to prevent the "domino effect" of sequential Asian countries becoming Communistic. It was widely believed that you were safe from deployment to Vietnam if you had less than a year of service time remaining. So the day I reached that date, Sally and I celebrated by putting the girls to bed early, opening a five-dollar bottle of wine, and enjoying a cozy evening.

In the army, I was not a surgeon. Instead they gave me three months of training reading X-rays and then classified me as a radiologist. Each morning my view box was covered with films. But the morning after Sally and I enjoyed our celebration of my "home free" status, instead of X-rays I found a short note on my view box: "The Colonel would like to see you immediately."

It felt as if I'd just been pushed off a cliff. I knew what this summons meant: I wasn't being honored with a military citation; I was being deployed to experience the hell that is war. I trudged through the long, dreary 1940s corridors of the sprawling hospital. A relic of World War II, it had been designed to withstand a direct hit by a bomb. In fact, it would have taken dozens and dozens of bombs to destroy it because the buildings were many and spread out. Once, summoned to the emergency room to treat a patient in cardiac arrest, I set out running. After a minute or two and with a long way still to go, I was forced to a slow jog. Finally, minutes later, sweating and gasping, I staggered into the emergency room. I was too late to save him.

The pathetically dilapidated building matched my emotions.

The Colonel was efficient, though I detected a faint hint of compassion. "Effective immediately," he said briskly, "you are to proceed to Ft. Hood, Texas, assigned to the 85th Evacuation Hospital." He didn't need to say where it was going. "You have ten days to relocate your family and report." He shook my hand. Should I salute? I felt like throwing up!

⤷

We packed our furniture and put it in storage. With our daughters Lynn, age three, and Ann, five months old, in the backseat, we headed from the Ozarks to civilization—if McKeesport, a rapidly shrinking steel town in western Pennsylvania, could be defined that way.

Two days later I headed to Texas. The takeoff from Pittsburgh was lift-you-out-of-your-seat rough, and for the first time ever, I contemplated death in a plane crash as a possible positive outcome.

Our hospital, the 85th Evacuation, had been decommissioned after World War II. That means that in July 1965, we were to practice medicine with equipment that dated back to the mid-1940s. There were thirty-five doctors and a similar number of nurses, none with a minute of combat experience. If we had an orientation meeting, I don't remember it. I couldn't then or now remember the names of three people I met at Ft. Hood.

All the nurses had volunteered. One was male; he was the arm-wrestling champion on staff. Many were either young or idealistic, often both; some were just excitedly looking forward to adventure. A few seemed to be trolling for doctors, or perhaps they were just naturally friendly. The docs were older. Some had young families. All had considerably less optimism than the nurses about returning in one piece.

After four or five days of meetings, boring beyond description, word spread that we had three-day passes before shipping out to Vietnam. There was a mass exodus from the base. Some took off to the local town with their new best friends (usually of the opposite sex, and sex was the operative word). The rest of us headed to the airport. Dressed in fatigues, soaked in sweat, I rushed to catch the next flight north, but despite my hurry I was late. The airport personnel were wheeling the stairs away and closing the plane's door as I ran out onto the tarmac. I pleaded with them, showed them pictures of my kids, begged, besought. Miracle of miracles, the crew rolled the steps back to the plane, opened the door, and led me to a seat in first class. I even got a round of applause. Patriotism was still a part of our national fabric in those early days of the war.

My day and a half at home was both wonderful and agonizing. Toddler Lynn couldn't understand why Daddy wouldn't be around for a while. Had she done something bad to make him leave? Five-month-old Ann just cuddled and cooed. I knew that when I returned, she wouldn't recognize me.

Then it dawned on me: Like most twenty-eight-year-olds, I didn't have a will. So a friend of the family produced one gratis, and a neighbor witnessed my signature. That didn't do much for Sally's morale, nor mine. I know that our second goodbye must have been far worse than the first, for the simple reason that I can't remember it at all—not one detail. I've repressed it completely.

Then it was El Paso to Oakland and the USNS *Barrett*. Next stop: Qui Nhon, Binh Dinh Province, Vietnam.

On board ship, we officers got tiny staterooms. The

five-thousand-plus enlisted men got bunks that they rotated in shifts every eight hours. Knowing my tendency toward seasickness, I'd swallowed a handful of Dramamine. *It worked!* I thought as I awoke next morning. *Not a hint of nausea!* Then I went on deck and discovered that we were still tied to the dock.

A few hours later, full of patriotism and apprehension, we sailed under the Golden Gate Bridge. To us would fall the honor of caring for those soldiers who would be shot, blown up—and by the end of our tour, those who were hooked on black-market drugs. All of this for the expressed goal of containing the spread of Communism.

The trip lasted three weeks, giving us time to begin to reorganize the hospital. Bill Burkhalter, our second-ranking officer, was career Army and an orthopedic surgeon. We had another orthopod, a short-timer, who was more interested in one of the nurses than in the mission at hand. We were to be a combat hospital of six to eight hundred beds, and 30 percent of the admissions were expected to be orthopedic casualties. We would be handling hundreds of casualties needing orthopedic surgery with each "push," the name we gave to those one- to two-day battles that characterized the war. But we had the equivalent of 1.5 surgeons to perform all those operations, sometimes three or four per patient!

Surprise, surprise—the Army might have miscalculated the staffing levels.

They asked for volunteers. My hand shot up. So did another across the room. Everyone else looked on in amazement. Didn't we know that you *never* volunteer for anything in the Army?

But I didn't see it that way—I was ecstatic. I had just secured the residency of my dreams! I would be working with Walter Blount, the surgeon who wrote the one and only book on children's fractures, which had revolutionized their care. He was famous as well for identifying Blount's disease, responsible for severe bowed legs in young children. (I would see epidemics of that condition forty years later in Africa.) The prospect of twelve months of orthopedic surgery, even if it was 99 percent trauma, suddenly made Vietnam a much more interesting proposition. I'd filled my duffel bag with orthopedic textbooks, hoping they'd be useful. Now they were mandatory. Mike, my newfound co-volunteer, would, like me, be returning to an ortho residency. Amazingly, it was the same one I was going to, and his father taught there.

We started our "informal" classes immediately with our private tutor, Colonel Bill. Topics included:

What's the circulation around the elbow? What nerves will be injured by a gunshot wound there?

Start with the brachial plexus and trace the ulnar nerve to the tip of the fourth finger.

What are the symptoms of "fat embolism"? How do you treat it?

Then we got the history of trauma surgery. Debridement in the modern sense (cutting away injured or infected tissue) was first used in the early nineteenth century by one of Napoleon's surgeons. Neglected wounds produced pus, which attracted flies, whose larvae "eat" dead tissue, which, amazingly, creates immaculately clean wounds. (The use of fly larvae was approved for such treatment by the FDA in 2004.) In the late nineteenth century, immobilization of the limb in a plaster cast was introduced to further facilitate healing.

Colonel Bill added the occasional aphorism, like "There are old surgeons. There are bold surgeons. But there are very few *bold old surgeons.*" Great advice when your patient has half a dozen holes in him. In that situation it translates as, Attack the many life-threatening injuries, but with a controlled caution.

We heard nothing during that training about what would prove to be one of the most common and long-lasting injuries of the Vietnam War and every other war in the modern era: post traumatic stress disorder.

We finally dropped anchor in Qui Nhon, Vietnam. The night before we disembarked I got a hint of what I was getting into: flashes of gold and orange ashore distinguished land from the dusky sky as faint rumbles welcomed us to a war zone. At the bottom of my duffel, beneath the anatomy and surgical texts, was my Bible. I flipped it open, hoping that the Lord might comfort me despite my years of irregular absence from his presence.

He did with Psalm 25:20: *Guard my life and rescue me; do not let me be put to shame, for I take refuge in you.*

He certainly performed the "guard" part, as I will explain. And because my skills as a trauma surgeon were developed by the carnage that was thrust upon us, "shame" was not a concern. *Exhaustion* and *frustrations,* yes, but not shame.

I climbed topside again. More rumbles sounded in the distance. "Our Father, who art in heaven . . ." I prayed quietly. Alone in the twilight on the gently heaving deck of the *Barrett*, I heard the ominous rumblings of war. "And deliver us from evil," my prayer continued.

But I couldn't imagine the evil I was about to see.

Next morning it was time to leave the *Barrett*, my now favorite ship. The first thing I noticed was that there were no disembarking piers, no ramps. It would be over the railing and crawling down webbing hung over the side of the ship. Was I really in the Marines? I felt as if I were in a John Wayne movie. Over the side I went and clung to the webbing for dear life. Forty feet below bobbed an LCU—a landing craft utility (I was already picking up the military jargon that would identify me as a combat soldier, at least to someone who didn't know better). Looking down to find the next foothold in the webbing, I couldn't help noticing that the closer I got, the less safe the bouncing LCU looked—and it hadn't looked very safe to begin with.

Once my mates and I had made it into the LCU and were crammed into every available space, the obvious question was whether you wanted to be in the front or the back when you hit the beach. If there was gunfire, the back was the obvious choice. Unlike in the movies, there was no heroic music in the background.

We powered onto the beach, ground to a halt in the sand, the front ramp dropped open, and out we came.

Despite the sounds of war the previous evening, this didn't exactly feel like landing in a war zone. Beautiful beaches stretched in both directions, populated by a few women in sarongs and cone straw hats, each carrying either food or a baby, usually both, on their back. Our arrival was a nonevent to these Vietnamese. A scraggly dog, happily wagging its tail in welcome, ran toward us. Before it reached us, a Vietnamese man, shovel in hand, casually cracked its skull, slung it over his shoulder, and carried it home for dinner, likely the first meat in weeks.

A "deuce-and-a-half truck" was the Army's answer to a taxi. We piled into the back and drove twenty kilometers to Phu Thanh, our home for the next month or so, where we were dumped in a Buddhist cemetery. Providential? Predictive? The surrounding hills looked peaceful, but they were held by Viet Cong.

Out came the canvas tents, then the shovels, then ropes, cots, and more tents. I kept wondering where the grunts were who would put up our tents. It turned out they had arrived with us—in fact, they *were* us.

"Doctor, would you prefer a pick or shovel to erect the tents, or a scythe to cut the grass?" someone asked.

I'd just heard that one of those using a scythe had inadvertently sliced the head off a coiled cobra. "Shovel will be fine," I said.

These beautiful beaches and seemingly peaceful hills camouflaged a deceptively violent land.

By evening we had erected only a couple tents and no cots, but exhaustion made sleep no problem. By the next evening, we had an ER and an OR tent, and I had blisters so bad I couldn't have scrubbed in for surgery to save my life ... or any life. The evening ended with my silent prayer, considerably longer than the sporadic prayers of my past. For the first time I could remember, I included, *Please guard my life.*

A day later a helicopter brought our first patient. His unshaven face was bloated to double normal size, weepy ooze glistening over it. Back at the air base in Qui Nhon, he'd walked in front of one of the fighter planes parked on the runway. The 120-degree heat on the tarmac had cooked off a rocket from beneath its wing. It had slit his throat, but the flaming exhaust had coagulated the bleeding. He'd been inches from being decapitated and inches from being unharmed. Doing his tracheotomy was easy, because his windpipe had already been opened by the rocket's fin.

As with 99 percent of our patients, I never knew what finally happened to him.

The valley wasn't safe; the Cong ruled once the sun set. We survived because we became their de facto battalion aid station. Most mornings, there would be one or two of their wounded lying at our perimeter. We would put them on a stretcher, bring them to the OR, and treat them just like our own. There was a biblical lesson in there somewhere. Probably a military one also.

The Cong could have overrun us whenever they wanted. That was obvious to us, but it was also obvious to General Westmoreland, the man in charge of all Vietnam forces. So he issued an order, and we changed places with a combat engineer group from Qui Nhon. Just to demonstrate who had been in charge, that first night the Cong attacked the engineers in our old haunt, and we treated their wounded.

Casualties continued to arrive sporadically. You might operate all day and through the night, then have nothing for five days. To combat boredom as much as anything, I volunteered at the provincial hospital because all their Vietnamese doctors had been conscripted by the military.

I would hitch a ride to the provincial hospital with one of our doctors who was also volunteering. When we arrived, the hospital administrator, deferentially bowing his head like a bobblehead doll, asked if we would take care of a young woman who needed a C-section. I had scrubbed on a few C-sections in medical school, so how hard could this be? Besides, I would just be assisting Bob, one of our best general surgeons.

I hadn't an inkling at the time that I was in fact preparing myself for the type of medicine and the operating conditions that I would many years later experience in mission hospitals in Africa.

We were given a sketchy history before we went into the OR. The young mother, about fourteen years old, fifteen at most, had been in labor for three days. Her family had brought her from the foothills to the coast and this regional government hospital in Qui Nhon. Neither Bob nor I had any experience in obstetrics; Bob had been doing transplant surgery research at Walter Reed before getting shipped over. But we were surgeons—or at least Bob was. It would have to be enough.

A technician put the rubber anesthesia mask over the patient's face, dialed 4 on the circa-1930 brass gauge on the anesthesia machine, and then screwed on the bottle of ether. A frayed tube conducted air to the patient's mask, creating an anesthetic mixture last common in 1910. He nodded for us to begin, then left the room. We—and the patient—were on our own.

As I remembered from med school, C-sections weren't usually complicated. But this mother's uterus was so thin and so close to the skin that you had to take care with your first incision so that it didn't slice through and cut the baby. Bob's incision to open our young mother's abdomen produced blood that was a light cherry pink instead of the deep burgundy of normal blood. I thought that perhaps the clear amniotic fluid was somehow diluting the blood.

Then I realized that the patient had been silently hemorrhaging during these long hours of futile labor, and her blood was so diluted that it was incapable of carrying oxygen to her baby ... or even to her.

But I was confused. Our first incision got us through the skin and muscle wall, but we hadn't opened the uterus—yet there the baby was, lying motionless among coils of his mother's small bowel, his tiny fingers still curled around the umbilical cord that was to have supplied him nutrition and oxygen. His eyes blankly looked into a world he would never experience. Sometime in the past three days, most likely within the past few hours, his mother's contractions had torn her uterus open, destroying the sanctuary that had up until then sustained his life. His brief life outside the womb, but still inside his mother's abdomen, was tranquil but doomed.

While I was still struggling to grasp the truth of the infant's death, our anesthesiologist returned—and frantically pointed to the blood pressure cuff, then his wrist, shaking his head.

No pulse! Our patient's heart had stopped.

Bob grabbed the scalpel again and made a gash over the left side of her chest. Within seconds he had his hand inside, squeezing her heart. The anesthesiologist pumped the bag that provided air to our patient's lungs. I could discern a pulse in her groin, but the vehicle necessary to transport the desperately needed oxygen to the heart—red blood cells—lay pooled in her abdomen. Calling for blood to transfuse her was not an option in this primitive hospital. We kept up the drill—Bob squeezing her heart, the anesthesiologist squeezing the air bag—for what seemed like ten or fifteen minutes. Time moves so slowly in these crises that it might have been less.

Whenever Bob paused, the young woman's pulse was undetectable. There wasn't a flicker of heart muscle activity.

So he stopped. The baby, lying motionless in her abdomen, was placed on his mother's breasts and a stained sheet placed over them.

A cacophony of crying erupted outside the door. Our anesthesiologist rushed to the doorway, prattling unintelligibly, waving his hands, pointing at us, then the baby, then back at us.

Then silence.

Then we heard a nearly inaudible murmuring in an unfamiliar

dialect, presumably that of their remote mountain home. I asked our anesthetist, "Is it a Buddhist prayer?"

"I think it is something about, 'All are nothing ... but flowers ... in a flowing ...'" He shook his head.

Then quiet. We waited, motionless.

I'm sure that Bob, like me, was wondering: How could they *not* assume that we were responsible for these deaths? After all, we had had her life—her very heart—in our hands. Were they going to accuse us of killing the mother and baby? There were Viet Cong posters plastered on the walls of their village that warned that the Americans brought death!

Were they armed? If nothing else, they would certainly have machetes. I had already, in my short time in Vietnam, sewed up the results of plenty of knife wounds, the result of too much beer and too few women.

This family had never even met us before the operation, and now two too-white Americans were standing over their dead daughter and grandson!

Not just mother and father but also aunts and uncles had been silently huddled in the hall as this catastrophe unfolded. Now, quietly, heads bowed, they walked into the OR.

Explanations were unnecessary. The silent figures of their daughter and dead grandson lying in this disarray of bloody drapes made clear what had happened.

The father was the first to move. He placed his hands together and brought them up to his head ... to attack us?

But then he bowed his head and bent deeply from the waist. A somewhat younger man next to him reverentially placed his hands together, brought them to his face, and bowed as well. Soon six or seven family members were doing the same thing.

In a soft whisper, they murmured something. Perhaps another Buddhist prayer?

Should we join them in prayer? A cultural Jew and a lapsed Methodist, sending these innocents to ... where?

I prayed silently: *"Father God, have mercy on these your children. Perhaps they never heard of your Son, but you are a God of comfort, so please extend that to these innocents."*

The men came alongside the OR table with the makeshift stretcher that they had used to bring our former patient on their long journey from the rice fields. They continued to murmur soft prayers, now also nodding their heads at Bob and me as they shuffled on the blood-splattered floor. Gently they picked up the silent remains of their daughter and grandson and slid them onto their homemade stretcher. Bowing toward us until they were out of sight, mumbling softly, they began the long walk home.

In a country overrun with death, this was one—no, two—too many. I was beginning to understand that there were simply too many ways to die in Vietnam, and that it was the young, not the old, who suffered the most.

One day many years later, as I did the second hip replacement of the morning, the anesthetist, his voice an octave higher than normal, asked. "How much longer do you have?" I was nearly finished, somewhat bored as this routine procedure was ending. No significant blood loss, no surprises, and no complications ... except that as the anesthetist quickly pointed out, the patient's heart had suddenly stopped! Resuscitation began immediately. A cardiac surgeon from the adjacent OR, who had just completed his case a few minutes previously, soon had the patient's chest open, squeezing his heart and injecting medicines directly into cardiac muscle. I stepped back to let these specialists do their magic.

Except that this time, the magic didn't work. The patient died. My immediate thought was of that young mother in Vietnam and her doomed baby.

What had I learned those many years before?

The answer: We don't have all the answers.

⤳

By November, having operated on a few hundred patients, I was gradually becoming a cautiously bold surgeon!

Our patients usually arrived by helicopter, so when our volleyball game was interrupted one day by a Huey touching down, it didn't seem out of the ordinary. Little did we realize that we were about to be part of one of the bloodiest battles of Vietnam, the Ia Drang Valley fiasco.

My first patient smelled bad. Most GIs coming off a patrol, without a bath in ten days, didn't smell like a bouquet of roses, but this was a different smell.

He had shit his pants. (Excuse my choice of words, but the more polite term of "messing" one's pants is what a nine-month-old baby or a senile nonagenarian does. There's nothing polite about a battlefield.)

He wasn't simply embarrassed by this—he was mortified! He was also in shock, so we needed to strip him down and find his gunshot wound, or perhaps the multiple fragment wounds from a grenade or land mine.

We threw out his shorts and washed his bottom.

And then discovered that there wasn't a mark on him. We looked for signs of a concussion injury or blunt trauma, but there weren't any. His blood pressure was shock-level low, so we put a cut-down in his cephalic vein—that is, we inserted a plastic tube that the needle is customarily attached to—and began delivering a quart of saline every minute. When patients have multiple wounds, blood loss is rapid and extreme, and replacement volume can total one or two times their normal blood volume, more than twenty units. The customary needle doesn't allow the massive amounts of fluid replacement that combat injuries require, so we dispensed with needles and placed the IV tubes directly into the veins.

Ten minutes later, the patient's pulse was still rapid, but his blood pressure was normal. As I left him to attend to another casualty, he was talking to an orderly in a hoarse whisper and shaking his head. His face was flushed, which didn't fit with his hypotension.

I pieced together his story only later, based on a few comments from the patient as well as some from his friends. He was a private in the 1st Battalion, 7th Air Cavalry, 1st Cavalry Division. He and two hundred or so of his buddies had been on what was euphemistically called a "search and destroy" mission in the Ia Drang Valley of the Central Highlands. Their helicopters set down in a deserted meadow called Landing Zone X-ray, a nice medical term that foreshadowed their fate. Not until their choppers had left did they discover that they had stumbled into a Viet Cong stronghold. They were outnumbered four or five to one. Hand-to-hand fighting ensued, and their position was overrun. After an hour or so, the 1st Cav acting CO made one last call: "We're overrun! Direct fire to this vector!"

My patient, surrounded, his ammunition exhausted, lay face down, simulating the death he expected any second. He couldn't see, but he could hear shouts, cries for mercy followed by the crack of a single shot, then high-pitched laughter and more shouting ... more shots and laughter.

He waited for the inevitable. A sudden kick to his chest rolled him partially over. His life depended on giving an Oscar-worthy impersonation of a dead GI. Despite his best performance, he felt a hot gun barrel thrust against his temple. He said a quick prayer, thought of his pregnant wife and the baby he'd never see ... and waited.

Click!

The Vietnamese soldier burst into raucous laughter; he was out of ammunition!

That's when my patient shit himself.

As his would-be assassin reloaded, a massive explosion signaled incoming "friendly" artillery. When the artillery onslaught finally subsided, there was absolute silence. Was he now alone? At least there was no further sound of laughter.

Was his enemy in a foxhole a few feet away? Had they fled the area? Would there be more incoming "friendly" fire, and would it annihilate him instead of the enemy?

Playing dead beat the real thing. So he waited, motionless. Finally he heard the distinctive *whap-whap* of arriving Chinook helicopters, come to salvage the wounded and extract those already dead. He was rolled onto a stretcher and shortly deposited at the 85th.

I prescribed a shower, some hot K rations, and the sight of our young nurses as all the treatment this soldier needed. A few days later, he hitched a ride back to Pleiku and his unit.

When I think back on that day, and especially on that young soldier, I ask myself a question that, at the time, we weren't asking: Had he already exhibited, and would he continue to experience, the symptoms of post-traumatic stress disorder (PTSD)? Symptoms such as persistent ringing in his ears? Erratic mood swings? Dizziness? Inability to sleep? Memory problems? Visual disturbances?

Odds are good that he—and a significant percentage of other soldiers who fought in that war—did have those symptoms. Would he ask for further medical care? I think it's safe to assume that there's a 99 percent chance he didn't. He would live with his "shame"—and he would rehash it over and over for years if not for the rest of his life.

It would be foolish to assume he was healed. How many nights would he waken in a cold sweat, having relived that real nightmare? How would his life change? Would he, like many other undiagnosed PTSD sufferers from that war, seek relief in drugs and alcohol?

Upon discharge, there would be nothing on his discharge papers to warn that this man had experienced a traumatic near-death experience that could—and almost inevitably would—result in serious psychological and behavioral effects later. If and when he became dysfunctional, he might just be categorized as a "deadbeat" or a "thug"; most likely, no one would guess at his true diagnosis, post-traumatic stress disorder.

And what would he think of himself? Would he recall that horrible day and think of himself as a coward? Would that cause him despair? Anger? Alcoholism? If so, it's unlikely that his wife would stay with him. Would his son ever know why his father wouldn't talk to him about the war?

But on the day I treated him and the rest of the Ia Drang injured, there wasn't time to speculate about their future. The casualties kept coming: dozens, then hundreds, muddy, in shock, parts of limbs missing. Our entire hospital was immersed in a casualty tidal wave of mortally injured young men. They stacked them outside each of the five ORs. We made our diagnoses as we cut their fatigues off. Our pre-op evaluations consisted of "I'll take this side, you take that." Some wounded arrived with a cut-down on each upper arm, supplying a unit of blood every two minutes.

It went on and on. Twelve hours. Eighteen hours. At twenty-four hours, I had gone from simply seeing the problem and reacting, to a fuzzy state where I had to s-l-o-w-l-y think through the situation and deliberately choose from among the options for what to do next. At thirty-two hours, I was outside my body, watching a stranger operate.

The colonel finally ordered me to bed. Exhausted, I lay looking at the ceiling. Four or five hours later, having gotten little or no actual sleep, I was back in the OR, cleaning up those with minor injuries—a relative term, since if you're the one with the injury, it's never minor.

A second wave of injured arrived forty-eight hours later. Their injuries were even worse, resulting from another ambush as they attempted to retreat to a more secure landing site. But as stressful as my ordeal was, I was aware that it was nothing compared to what my patients were going through: Viet Cong suicide soldiers crawling into our American camp, high explosives strapped to their bodies, willing to die in order to take enemy soldiers with them. Then the enemy booby-trapped our dead or wounded so that one more American might be killed as we attempted to leave no soldier behind, dead or alive.

Medal of Honor recipient Major Bruce Crandall was one of many brave chopper pilots who risked their lives dozens of times, in his case twenty-two times, ferrying the wounded from the murderous battle to our hospital. Again and again I saw exhausted medics giving every ounce they had to care for the young men who had been wounded. My patients averaged nineteen years old, and they survived, even though many of them were terribly maimed. At least they were not among the more than 58,000 Americans who ultimately lost their lives in that twenty-year-long war.

～

Lurking at the back of my mind in the days—and even years—following that ordeal was the question: *Could I have done a better job?* How long did I carry that question? I don't know, but even now, writing about it brings tears to my eyes.

We received more than three hundred wounded from that battle. A similar number went directly to the morgue. In those early days of the Vietnam conflict, American dead began to reach a thousand per month.

But those were the visible casualties. We can't forget the tens or hundreds of thousands of "invisible" casualties. Around 2.7 million Americans served in South Vietnam. Although we didn't talk about PTSD in those days, it's estimated now that 10, 15, or maybe more than 20 percent of the combat soldiers in that (or any) modern war eventually suffered from PTSD. Many will never know they have it. They are just depressed and don't know why. A hair-trigger anger now clouds too many days and destroys too many families.

Soldiers, and that includes me, can't help being changed by the hell of war. It's not a sign of weakness. In the Civil War, by far the costliest American war in terms of casualties, they called the emotional effects *soldier's heart.* In World War I, it was described as *shell shock.* In World War II, *battle fatigue* was rampant in the European campaigns but, interestingly, rare in the Pacific, where battles were usually concluded in days or a few weeks.

Kijabe, God's answer to my prayers.

Although the sign calls it an orthopedic hospital, it became primarily a neurosurgical hospital that revolutionized the treatment of hydrocephalus, i.e. water on the brain, in thirty-seven countries (and counting) worldwide.

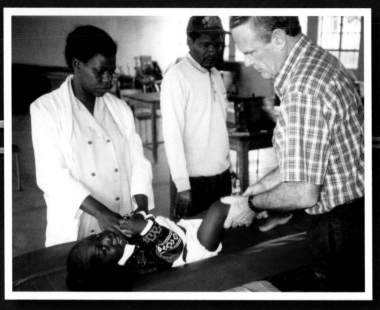

His hip slid in and out of joint. Surgery corrected it.

*The first of hundreds of thousands
of club feet treated at CURE facilties.*

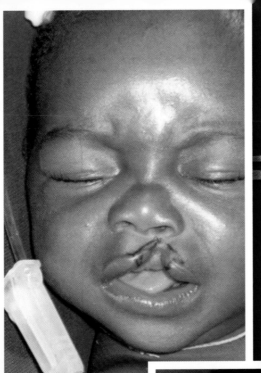

Cleft lips, seemingly an epidemic in Africa.

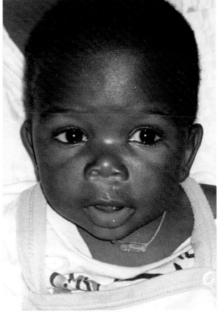

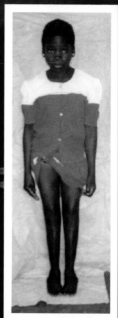

Blount's disease, i.e. congenital genu varus,
initially described in the 1930s
by my professor, Walter Blount.

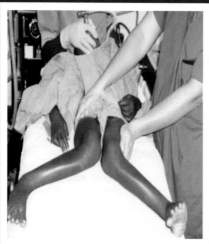
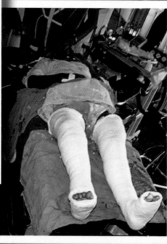

*Genu valgus, even
more disabling.*

Only after his legs were straight, and therefore no longer "cursed," would his father acknowledge his son.

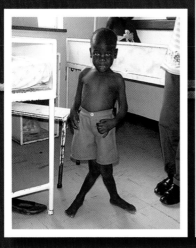

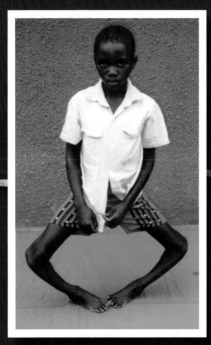

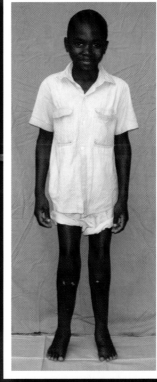

Look at his face, not his legs.

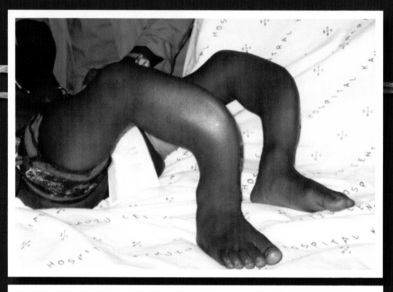

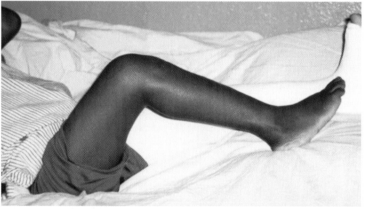

The scarcity of health care enabled this treatable
deformity to become extremely disabling.

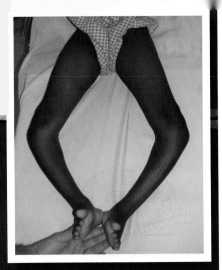
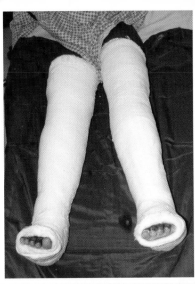

*Without corrective surgery, no hope for
schooling, a job, a wife, or a family.*

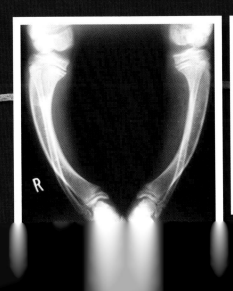
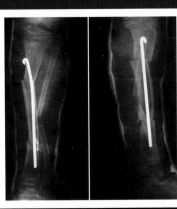

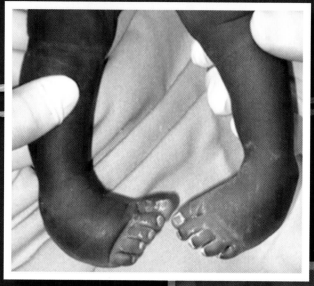

One of the more than
100,000 children cured!

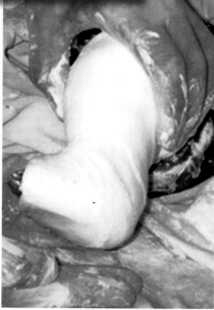

The Department of Defense estimates that some 13 to 20 percent of the men and women who have served in Iraq and Afghanistan will develop or already have PTSD. That's between 330,000 and 520,000 men and women. The major symptom is depression; others are anxiety, panic, insomnia, flashbacks, sadness, inability to focus, and self-blame. And since our bodies are connected to our minds, physical symptoms also occur: hypertension, respiratory problems, and chronic physical pain. Self-medication with alcohol or drugs is common, and tragically, suicide is a frequent outcome. In the current war against terrorism, it has been estimated that for every soldier killed in combat, twenty-five will die from suicide.

Staggering—especially considering that, serving as a doctor in America's fourth costliest war, I made a diagnosis of PTSD only once in the whole year I was there.

And me? Did I experience PTSD? Certainly I was changed by my war experience. I became hot-tempered and combative, especially about the fact that we Vietnam War veterans were treated as scum upon our return, as if we were a disgrace. (I still sometimes see that disgust when people find out that I served in Nam.)

It wasn't until forty years later that anyone publicly thanked me for serving my country in that conflict. It was during a Memorial Day church service.

I cried.

So ... maybe, just maybe, I *did* have a touch of PTSD.

Otherwise, maybe I'd be able to forget the captain who looked so much like me we could have been twins. His head wound was catastrophic but not immediately fatal. I watched him lie on a stretcher most of the night. His last breath came shortly before sunrise.

And soldiers weren't the only failures that sear my memory. There was the ten-year-old who was riding his bike in the village of Qui Nhon when a speeding jeep hit him broadside only a few feet from where I stood. I explained to the shaken driver that I worked at the 85th and persuaded him to take us both to the ER. The child, in shock, had bruises on his chest and abdomen. His upper left abdominal quadrant was exquisitely tender, a textbook ruptured spleen. A few units of blood to stabilize his pressure, removal of his spleen, and he'd be back on a bike in a few weeks.

Except there was no blood available. We had just completed one of those "pushes" as we referred to an onslaught of wounded GIs with multiple wounds. The few units of blood that remained needed to be kept available in case we received stragglers. The treatment of injured soldiers came first.

I stayed by his cot in the ER all night, pouring saline into the antecubital vein in his arm while his ruptured spleen filled his distending abdomen with his life's blood.

All I could do was pray for my tiny Buddhist friend that somehow the pressure of the buildup of blood in his abdominal cavity might control his hemorrhage.

He slowly lost consciousness. He too died shortly before sunup.

As I left the hospital, I looked up to heaven and asked—no, screamed—"Did that boy really have to die? If he had to be hit, couldn't it have been on a day when we had blood to give him?"

And there above me, at 45,000 feet, high enough that the enemy's SAM missiles couldn't reach them, were the B-52 Stratofortresses, the predawn sun injecting ominous scarlet into their ethereal white vapor trails, bringing their 70,000-pound daily dose of death to the Viet Cong, as well as, sadly, to their mothers and sisters.

In the quiet of the early dawn, I nodded and thought again what I had thought on my first day in this war, hoping to avoid cobras as we prepared our sleeping tents: *This is a deceptively violent place.*

I was sure I wouldn't be the only one praying this day—the boy's mother would be praying also. Would we even be able to find her? Would she ever know for sure what had happened to her son?

Does a mother who suddenly loses a young son experience PTSD?

⟿

PTSD is often associated with guilt. Survivor's guilt, for instance, when a soldier is the only one from his platoon who survives the battle—as with my young patient who survived the battle of Ia Drang by playing dead.

Or my own sense of guilt at being unable to save the young mother and her doomed unborn who made the three-day trip to the Quin Yon hospital. It wasn't simply that we'd been unable to save her. It was also that we, the American forces, had inadvertently eliminated her access to health care locally. It hadn't been deliberate, but it had nevertheless caused her fatal three-day journey.

I was acutely aware that I was maturing as a surgeon. And perhaps as a man.

The guilt associated with PTSD occasionally finds a unique resolution. John Plummer was a Vietnam chopper pilot ordered to destroy a small village with napalm. A photograph of one of the survivors of that attack, taken immediately after John's assault, showed a nine-year-old girl fleeing down the road naked, with burns on her chest and outstretched arms, her open mouth silently shouting her anguish. That image was riveted in John's mind in the same way that some of my own most vivid memories of Nam have been riveted in mine. That and other memories overwhelmed him; his PTSD was catastrophic. As happens so often with PTSD, he sought solace in booze, which led to the death of his marriage.

Thirty years later, he attended a memorial service at the Vietnam Veterans Memorial in Washington, DC. To his amazement, a woman on the platform, Phan Thi Kim Phuc, was introduced as the girl in the picture … the girl he had branded with napalm.

Sobbing, he introduced himself as the one who had destroyed her village and inflicted her scars. Rather than seeking vengeance, she embraced him and whispered, "I forgive you." Her forgiveness was the healing potion he needed to be healed of his PTSD.

Seldom can PTSD be resolved so dramatically, so completely.

Patients aren't the only ones affected by their medical conditions; those giving the care are affected as well. It's difficult to be both the doctor and the patient, but all physicians and surgeons are called upon to do just that. Caring for more than a thousand wounded GIs changed me in many ways, some I'd have been happy to avoid. But I am thankful that in that intense experience, I learned to meld a *prudent caution* with a *measured aggression*.

CHAPTER 10

LEWIS

COMPARE THE PRACTICE OF AN ORTHOPEDIC SURGEON TO that of an oncologist or geriatric specialist. One big difference: death is not a common part of an orthopedic surgeon's practice. But when I began practicing in Africa, that changed drastically. I began seeing patients with life-threatening spinal cord injuries, malignant tumors that were often hopelessly advanced, and diseases rare in the developed world but very common in this land of poor nutrition and hygiene. Actually, those injuries and diseases weren't just life *threatening*—they were a virtual guarantee of an early end of life.

And in 1986 my first patient, Lewis, on my first day of my first stint performing surgery in Africa was the beginning of a parade of such patients.

Lewis dragged himself into the shabby examining room in the Queen Elizabeth Hospital, Blantyre, Malawi, known somewhat fondly as the QE2. He had arrived with the aid of a "bush crutch," meaning a scraggly tree limb. He held it diagonally across his chest, planting the end of it against the ground a foot or so in front of him and then dragging himself up to it. His bare feet scraped across the floor, his knees braced together in a semi crouch. The effort to move even a few yards was so exhausting that sweat dripped from his brow.

The coat of his well-worn suit nearly touched his knees, and his hands hung well below them. The collar of his white shirt was three sizes too large—at least it was now, in his emaciated condition. But his tie was clean, the Windsor knot correctly tied, a small emblem with initials on it a few inches below. Though his neck jutted forward, his head tilted back to compensate for his hunchback-like deformity. His expression was stoic, except for his eyes, which were filled with intensity—or was that fear?

"He's your only patient today," explained Ed, the sometime-surgeon who had invited me to Malawi in the first place. "Despite all the crippled kids in this country, I couldn't find any pediatric spine cases for you. They all seem to croak. Parents tend to just keep them at home rather than bringing them to the hospital, since they know there's nothing to be done. But just a few days ago, Lewis dragged himself into the ER begging for help."

Lewis pulled himself over to where I sat, stood as close to upright as he could manage, and announced, "So you are the American doctor that has come to fix my legs." The look in his eyes, I could see now, was clearly fear. But his expression also showed a trace of a smile.

He handed me a rolled-up X-ray of his twisted spine; a quick glance at it revealed three tuberculous vertebrae crushed into a gnarled heap. I would be operating on Lewis without benefit of an MRI, or CT, or even an old-fashioned myelogram; this crinkled X-ray was all the diagnostic test I would have. This surgery would be freehand. How good was my imagination, trying to envision what we would find?

"Make me walk again!" Lewis said as a statement, not a

question. He seemed to have no doubt, but I sure did! Once again, I detected the hint of a smile as he nodded his head, as if we shared a secret joke.

He wasn't asking *if* I could heal him. He was announcing that I *would*. Lewis's faith that a doctor from America could work miracles was unshakable. And a miracle was what he needed.

Working hard at maintaining his balance, he told me his story: "Just three months ago, my body was normal. I was able to play soccer with my nine children. Then I began to notice problems at work—I'm a conductor for the Rift Valley Railway. I had trouble climbing back onto the rail cars. I assumed it was just soreness from running with my boys."

He paused, perspiration beading on his forehead. He tipped forward, and I grabbed him before he fell. "It keeps getting worse," he said. "I now have trouble making my water. And then—" he stopped, his eyes pleading for understanding— "I could no longer do my duty as a husband."

He collapsed, and I half dragged him to the examination table. Testing for sensation revealed that his spine was compromised at the sixth thoracic level. His reflexes were hyperkinetic, a reflection of lack of direct nerve control.

Soon his bowel and bladder control would fail, and he would need a diaper. Without protective sensation, he would develop pressure sores on his feet and legs. The only relief he would find would be death from urinary sepsis.

"I'm on sick leave from my job," he said, "but that will end soon. When I can't return to my job at the railroad, I will lose it. Then I will have no health insurance, no disability income." He stared over my shoulder, as if envisioning the utter destruction of his family. No money for school fees, so no further education for his children. With unemployment at 40 to 60 percent, what chance would children without education have at meaningful jobs?

He knew what this meant for his daughters. The night streets were polluted with unemployable girls, especially on the weekends. This new disease, AIDS, would be their destiny. No jobs meant that the cycle of poverty, which his family had endured for centuries, would continue. The future of two generations would be devastated if we couldn't restore strength to his legs!

"I'll do what I can, Lewis," I said. "But so many things can go wrong in these circumstances. I would list them for you, but most you won't understand—and besides, the alternative to surgery is unacceptable, so we'll have to try."

That ended our meeting.

The odds for Lewis were poor to begin with, but then they got worse. "I can't allow this surgery you're planning!" the head of surgery, a tall caricature of the noble Brit, said, stopping me in the hall. "I just won't have it. No one has ever done successful anterior spine surgery at this hospital. You have no idea how difficult it is to do *any* surgery here. No. No! It just won't do. Absolutely no such surgery here."

What I was proposing to do was to open the patient's chest, retract aside his heart and lungs, and then remove—using whatever equipment they had—his sixth, seventh, and eighth vertebrae. I'd scrape out the dead bone, remove the tuberculous abscess that was pressing against his spinal cord, and fill the gap with bone fragments from the ribs adjacent to my incision.

"In that case," I said to the Brit, "you will need to physically block me from wheeling Lewis into that OR. I didn't fly halfway around the world to watch this man's life end for lack of care we could have provided!"

I'd brought with me from America the basic surgical

equipment I needed. The hospital had a blood bank, so I ordered the four units I estimated Lewis might lose.

I'd operated on many children who needed this procedure. An adult would be easier in some ways, but in others more difficult because of the distortion of his anatomy from the silent ravages of the tuberculosis (TB) bacilli over a period of years.

As I made rounds later in the day, Lewis said, "I know you will heal me, doctor. I told my wife about you. She agrees—you will heal me!"

Was he trying to convince me or himself? His life, as well as his wife's and children's future, were now in the hands of a surgeon he'd known for twenty-four hours. "The operating rooms are temporarily down," I said, "but it will take a couple of days to get everything ready anyway."

And then the rest of our lives to live with the result.

The hospital where I was to perform this miracle, the QE2, had been built during the colonial period, before penicillin. Ether was still the anesthetic of choice. Patients as seriously ill or injured as Louis were usually all given the same treatment: *masterful neglect.* They put them to bed to die.

QE2 was a sprawling labyrinth of halls and wards interspersed with patches of bare ground; it seemed to have been designed as an amusement park maze. Families camped in the dirt strips between the wards, tending their small cooking fires while hanging their wash—as well as the patient's—to dry. The hospital held about 1,200 patients.

Later I discovered that there was a modern hospital only about a mile away from QE2 but separated by a century of medical progress and not available to those who couldn't pay in advance.

The next day, I met the hospital's three orthopedic registrars.

Their backgrounds were plumber, cab driver, and helper on the family farm plot. But their contagious enthusiasm gave me the first emotional lift of the trip. They had taken exams to be clinical officers. Today we'd call them physician assistants. These three were the brightest of the hundreds who'd taken the entrance exams

"Why don't you take Dr. Harrison on ward rounds?" Ed suggested.

Off we went: Hastings, who proudly told me he was of the Chewa tribe; Nyasa, who told me his name meant *lake* in his Yao language; and Mussa, who rarely said a word—he kept his head bowed and avoided eye contact. There were no chart racks, just a paper or two lying on each bed.

No nurse attended us on our rounds. There was, in fact, only one nurse for 104 patients, and our nurse was too busy passing out meds, identifying those experiencing relapses of their malaria or their intestinal parasites, or attending to a patient terminally ill from a yet-to-be-diagnosed condition. But my guides seemed to have been doing their job to the best of their ability. They knew each of the patients. Some were pre-op, and we discussed treatment options. Some were post-op, most of them lying on stained sheets, others on bare mattresses, some on beds, the majority on the floor.

I smelled one of them before I saw him. That sweet odor of gas gangrene was something I had first learned to recognize in Vietnam. It is morbidly pungent. And it is totally different from the rotting-garbage odor associated with a routine two-day-old gunshot wound or post-op infection.

Working the smell like an English setter, I oriented myself. "There," I said, pointing to a man hanging in skeletal traction two bed rows over, "is a man who'll be dead in twenty-four hours."

"He was bitten by a croc," Hastings informed me. "You know how they roll their prey in the water to kill them? His femur snapped when the croc spun him."

"Why hasn't he been operated on? Let's get him to the OR!" I said—and then remembered: The ORs were down.

My assistants reminded me of that in a mumble, eyes to the ground. "None of the sterilizers work."

Okay, then. "Can we take him to another hospital?"

They brightened up—but only for a second. "We don't have any transport. The ambulance hasn't worked in a few weeks. They're waiting for a part from South Africa."

"Is there a pickup truck? We can lay him in the back," I said, grasping at straws. That brought the enthusiasm back. A series of phone calls found a mission hospital twenty miles away with an OR available the next morning. If we brought our own instruments, we could use it.

Mussa's uncle volunteered his pickup, cautioning that it sometimes didn't start. It would have to do.

"I doubt he'll make it till then," I muttered, and no one disagreed.

But 6:30 the next morning found us bouncing along a dirt road. My team, now affectionately known as "the boys," were riding in the back, one pulling on the pin in our patient's tibia in a vain attempt at stabilizing the fractured femur, with another pulling in the opposite direction by grabbing him under the arms. You might call it a form of mobile traction! Fortunately our patient, who had initially grimaced and moaned at each pothole, had finally lapsed into a coma.

The hospital, once we got there, seemed vacant. The boys took charge. After laying the stretcher on an OR table that dated, I'm sure, from the 1930s, one of my boys assumed the role of anesthetist, sitting at the head of the table fussing with some 1950s-era anesthesia equipment. He soon had our victim/patient anesthetized. It didn't take much, since the patient had been in a toxic coma. Another of my boys prepped the leg while the third member was scrubbing with me.

"Have you ever done an AK amp?" I began. (That's ortho-speak for "above the knee amputation.") I went on without waiting for the answer. "I'm planning on having you do the surgery. Your buddy can join us to assist. Until then, I'll be your first assistant." Because of his surgical mask, I couldn't tell what his reaction was, but I was pretty sure I saw his knees shaking.

With false bravado, I announced, "Gentlemen, if he survives the next twenty minutes, this man will be awake and eating dinner tonight! You won't believe how fast a young guy like this can recover once we stop this poison from killing him."

I think I lost them with that prediction. They had seen way too many croc bites. They knew better. Croc bite victims don't survive. This drill, they assumed, was just to appease the enthusiastic American surgeon who didn't know any better, and to give them some training in advanced surgical techniques. For my part, after seeing way too many high-velocity gunshot wounds in Vietnam, I had a lot of faith in the recuperative ability of the human body, especially a young body.

As surgery began, I was impressed by my boys. They already functioned as a team. I would discover later that they rotated the roles each would play so that all got to do surgery and anesthesia and function as scrub nurses. Although no American hospital would allow that, it was the only way to function in this poorest country in the world.

Perhaps, I thought, *American surgeons might be more understanding if they served as scrub nurses from time to time.*

Our patient's wound was seriously infected, so we kept cutting away the tissue until there was no sign of infected or ischemic tissue to harbor *Clostridium tetani*, the bacterium that causes tetanus. We would leave the wound open to encourage drainage.

Then it was time for the amputation. In an American hospital, we'd likely have been able to save our patient's lower leg. We'd have had the equipment and the skills to reconstruct the femur, and there would have been follow-up care. But this was Malawi. And we were trying to save a life. So off came the leg.

One of the least appetizing events in an OR is passing off an amputated limb. This was no exception: splat, it was just thrown on the floor—there was no one to hand it to. We applied a bulky dressing. I added a silent prayer.

Soon we were on our way back to the QE2. Our patient, in the back of the truck again, was now very much alive, but mumbling about the pain in his leg that we had left in the garbage can.

I couldn't hide my pride when we made rounds that night and saw our patient eating dinner. I felt like my first day of surgery had been a win, even if our patient was upset that he no longer had a left leg.

I couldn't remember the last time I'd saved a life. If this was the highlight of my entire six weeks, I would be able to say it was worth it! And it validated my prayers these past few years about my desire to do mission surgery. Even if I never met another patient whose life I could save … and then it struck me that, in speaking of myself as the lifesaver, I was taking too much credit. Sally had been praying for this nameless man. We were a team—the three of us: the surgeon, the praying anchoress, and the Healer. I would remember to thank him tonight and then again tomorrow morning, before and after operating on Lewis.

Also, I was now confident that I would be allowed to do the

surgery. A young British anesthesiologist had just arrived, courtesy of the UK National Health Service. He and I had talked the day before about whether we could do this First World operation under these Third World conditions, and he had agreed that it was worth the risk. In most places, anesthetists' opinions trump surgeons' opinions, at least in the OR. Together we had rummaged through the dusty OR supply closet, which could have passed for a museum of antique medical instruments.

"Eureka!" he had shouted. "I've found a split endotracheal tube!" As he waved this bifurcated airway tube jubilantly above his head, we were both horrified to watch it crumble in his hands. It had probably lain on that shelf for twenty years. Apparently, I'd be doing this surgery with a thirty-year-old anesthesiologist but fifty-year-old equipment.

Sally and I had begun praying exhaustively for Lewis as soon as it became clear that the surgery would proceed. We had stumbled upon a verse that said, "Whatever you ask for in prayer, believe that you have received it, and it will be yours" (Mark 11:24 NIV). The word *believe* in that verse is in the present tense.

I usually pray in the *future* tense, hoping God will answer. But this verse commanded a present-tense level of belief, a conviction that what we were praying for—the healing of Lewis's paralysis—would happen. This verse didn't encourage the usual conditional belief: "If it is in your will, God." Rather, it encouraged simple, childlike certainty.

That challenged our faith. It seemed presumptuous. Like most Christians, we prayed for many things with the hope, even occasionally the expectation, that our prayer would be answered. But that was not what this verse had challenged us to do. It was a strong command not to *hope* but to *believe*. Sally and I made a pact that I wouldn't go ahead with this surgery unless both of us felt, and felt for certain, that God would heal Lewis.

By the next morning, we both had found that confidence. We both honestly believed God would heal Lewis. Not just that he could ... but that he positively *would*.

We had been able to get only two units of blood, rather than the four I had requested. As we began the surgery, I was focused on opening Lewis's chest. Then I looked up to a sea of nurses, aides, maintenance men, lab techs, and two orderlies who'd been mopping the OR next door. Everyone wanted to see what the excitement was about. And they all had one thing in common: They wore their masks at half mast, settled comfortably below their noses. Sure, they could breathe better this way, but the arrangement guaranteed that any and all bacteria in their noses had free access to the inside of my patient's chest. A couple of older missionary doctors who practiced in the hospital (possibly trained before the germ theory of disease was accepted) didn't bother with shoe covers either. Shaking their heads, they mumbled, "Does he understand where he is? We just don't do that sort of surgery here."

From the moment my scalpel touched Lewis's skin, bugs were a nuisance. They were the usual flying critters you expect at a Sunday picnic, only jumbo-sized for Africa. But this was most assuredly no picnic. The operating room was a relic of colonial days. There was no air conditioning, no fans, no screens at the open windows. I spotted a few lovely butterflies and at least one wasp the size of my thumb. I couldn't remember a lecture in American med school on how to handle insect life in the OR. Spraying the open chest cavity with insecticide would likely be fatal, but to my patient rather than the insects. A fly swatter appeared, but the well-intentioned orderly connected with more onlookers than bugs. I called for an armistice. The bugs were clearly winning. It was their picnic.

And it wasn't potato salad and hamburgers that attracted them. It was the beating heart of our patient. But they couldn't get to it, since it was surrounded by his collapsing left lung. Taking out Lewis's rib and detaching his diaphragm provided a great opportunity for an anatomy lesson. His aorta pulsated ominously. Slightly behind this, looking innocent, was the vena cava, the main vein that collects blood from the lower part of the body. And south of that, our abundant audience had a view of the spleen, and over there the tip of the liver, plus all those many feet of intestine.

They were all there, craning their necks to see. They might as well learn something, so I began my lecture: "See all those black flecks? That's what happens to your lungs when you smoke." But in Lewis's case, it was more likely caused by growing up tending the cooking fires used to prepare dinner.

"Here is his spine." I pointed to the gnarled mess, looking more like the exposed root of an old tree. "During his teenage years it was ravaged by tuberculosis."

Actually, Lewis was one of the lucky ones who had been able to get medication, which had cured the TB—but not before the disease had destroyed two or three of his vertebrae. Inexorably, over time, the bone had crumbled. Now, twenty years later, it was crushing his spinal cord, preventing the transmission of messages from his brain to his legs.

This surgery would proceed with no spinal cord monitoring to assure the safety of his spinal cord. No sophisticated monitoring of blood loss—just a negotiation between the surgeon and anesthesiologist: "Doesn't look like he's losing that much." No controlled hypotension to reduce the blood loss by half. No …

well, you get the idea. We were trying to do late-twentieth-century surgery with pre-World War II technology.

My young anesthesiologist remained ever optimistic. "Just do it the old-fashioned way," he suggested with that lovely Cockney accent. "Pack the lungs out of the way with whatever towels you can find. That ought to give you adequate exposure to the spinal cord. I'll just have to pump a little harder on the bag, but this chap should get through this just fine."

It was his fourth day working in the Third World. It was my second day.

My three young assistants couldn't stop asking questions.

Them: "So will the heart be all right pushed aside like that?"

Me: "Yes, it takes a lot to damage that muscle. It's the hardest-working muscle in your body."

Them: "Will all those black spots in his lung kill him?"

Me: "Well, they certainly aren't doing him any good. But I bet Lewis is exposed to a lot more dangers than secondhand campfire smoke. If we can get him walking again, he's more likely to be killed by a car on your narrow African roads than he is to be killed by cancer."

Them: "So that big tube full of blood—is that his aorta?"

Me: "No, that's the vena cava. Its walls are thin. If he's going to die in this operation, most likely it will be because we inadvertently nick that thing and it starts bleeding, and we can't find a way to stop it. Here, look behind—see that pulsing tube? That's his aorta. But the casing around it is strong, and it's unlikely that we'll puncture that."

(Back in the States, with the precision instruments that I would normally use, I could have made that assurance with confidence. Here at QE2, I was using chisels and gouges more suitable for making furniture than doing delicate spine surgery. My assistants seemed to find the statement reassuring.)

Me: "See these little vessels coming from the aorta that we keep slicing in two and tying off the ends, to gain access to the spine? These little ones are actually more likely to create a fatal complication. If even one of the dozens we tie breaks loose post-op, he will die of blood loss."

Just then an insect the size of a helicopter dived into the wound. The last time I had seen a bug that big in a wound was in Vietnam. One of my young helpers reached in and plucked the bug out.

"Okay," I said, looking at the gnarled mass of bone that had once been three vertebrae. "Now the real fun begins." I took one of the curved gouges and began, as gently as I could, hammering against his deformed spine. Instead of a gentle 40-degree curve, Lewis's spine was contorted at more than 100 degrees. On the far side of this twisted mass of bone was his buckled and squashed spinal cord. Finding it before I severed it with one of these chisels was the object of this exercise.

The normal spinal anatomy had been destroyed many years before by Lewis's TB. Starting at the edge of what seemed to be a normal vertebra, I chipped away until suddenly I uncovered an unexpected clump of yellow fibrous tissue. *That looks like the remnant of a disc,* I thought. *What is it doing there?* Then I realized that the bone on both sides of this disc had so deteriorated that two discs were adjacent to each other without the intervening vertebral body. With a shock, I realized that the usual anatomical landmarks couldn't be relied on in this operation. It would be like walking in the darkest of nights, trying to feel my way along the edge of a cliff.

We picked out the distorted fragments of bone. Lewis's spinal cord came into view one millimeter at a time. It had been so compressed by the crushed vertebra that it was totally disfigured. It should have been conical, and pulsating with each beat of the heart. But the more of the cord we uncovered, the more it resembled a flat Christmas ribbon. The conical shape had been slowly flattened by years of steady compression. Had the injury occurred suddenly, he would have been immediately paralyzed. But the body can adapt if the changes forced upon it are incremental, in stages. *How in the world can Lewis even feel his toes?* I wondered. That morning, when I'd done my final neurologic check, he could barely move his toes, but his sensation had been normal.

Giggles and whispering came from behind me as the nurses marveled at what they were seeing. It was standing room only in the OR. No wonder the bugs kept flying in: All the windows had been opened in an attempt to cool the room. It was a vain attempt—we were all sweating now.

From the condition of Lewis's deformity, I knew *what* was coming: The cord would suddenly be heading 90 degrees in the opposite direction. I just didn't know *when* that sharp turn would appear. If I found it one millimeter too late, I would inadvertently complete the destruction that the crushed spinal column had been creating.

An unusually large chunk of bone suddenly came loose as my gouge probed along the anterior spinal cord. "There it is!" I shouted. "That's the apex of the deformity. Now the really hard part starts, because the spinal column is coming toward us. We'll have to change tactics." I put down the gouge and switched to the ancient curettes. Using them to remove bone would require more strength, but it was the only safe way to peel the bone away with the cord now headed toward us.

And besides—the more desperate the situation, the stronger I become. Must be adrenaline.

A drop of water fell into the wound. I looked around to see what was happening and realized it was my own sweat. I had joined forces with the contaminators! "I need a sponge," I said to the nurse. She put it in my hand. I pointed to my forehead. "Sponge off my forehead and then throw it on the floor."

She hesitantly dabbed at my forehead. "Harder," I said. "He's only going to survive so much of this septic environment before all the antibiotics in Africa won't save him."

Three hours of this painstaking and strenuous work went on before we got to the end of the area of compression. It was only about four inches long, but Lewis's anatomy was so distorted that I couldn't begin to estimate how many vertebrae we had removed. I turned to one of the OR nurses and said, "Let me have that rib I took out at the beginning of the operation."

Her blank stare alarmed me. Had she thrown it away, not knowing that without it we couldn't complete the operation? I panicked for an instant. Our patient would never stand, let alone walk again!

She began muddling through the bloody clamps, chisels, curettes, and bloody rags that passed for sponges. Bulky instruments manufactured decades ago were piled in a heap. Finally, under a malleable retractor, she found my patient's rib.

"Well, God made a woman out of Adam's rib, let's see if we can make a few new vertebral bodies for Lewis from this one," I muttered half aloud. Nobody laughed, but sometimes people don't get surgical humor.

With the "nibblers," as the Brits call them, I began creating slivers of bone that looked more like wooden matchsticks than vertebrae. As I packed them around the gaping hole we had just meticulously created, I explained to the young doctors, "In three months this will become a solid bridge preventing any further collapse of Lewis's spine." *But, I thought, that will only happen if the inevitable infection isn't too serious and if he doesn't die from bed sores and* . . The number of possible complications racing through my mind seemed endless.

I recognized from my dwindling audience that the rest of the operation appeared to be anticlimactic. It certainly wasn't for me. Putting Lewis back together was going to be every bit as hard as opening him up, just not as dramatic. First we sewed what was left of the pleura (the membrane that surrounds the lungs) back over the matchstick "vertebrae." Allowing the lungs to reinflate is always a marvelous sight. As the anesthesiologist squeezed the antiquated black bag, the crumpled mass of lungs began unfolding. Each breath allowed for increasing size as the speckled lung gradually resumed shape. Inch by inch it covered up the beating heart, and with the last squeeze of the bag, the lungs reoccupied the left side of Lewis's deformed chest. I had brought some chest tubes with me, so Lewis was now the proud owner of a world-class, first-rate American chest tube.

But what to connect it to? Things routine in a First World hospital, such as postoperative suction and a closed system of drainage, were not available here. Instead we added six feet of tubing and made multiple serpentine loops, creating air fluid levels to prevent the collapse of his lungs.

Ingenious? Maybe. Effective? We would soon find out.

Perhaps one of the reasons no patients had survived this operation in Malawi was that there was no post-op care area in the hospital and no intensive care unit either. Lewis was wheeled right back to the fifty-bed orthopedic ward that now held 106 patients. Some beds accommodated two patients; some patients slept under a bed. I had pulled rank to get Lewis his own bed adjacent to the nurses' station. The nurse was responsible for all 106 patients, so she had no time to spare, but she would at least need to pass by Lewis as she cared for the other patients. If things started to go really wrong, it would happen right before her eyes. He was asleep when I left.

I had trouble unwinding when I got home. Even though six-hour operations are exhausting, it is also difficult to turn off your engine, which has been redlined all that time. I picked at my dinner and couldn't concentrate. My fatigue was bone deep, but I kept rehashing the surgery in my mind.

Before bed, I went back to the hospital to check on Lewis. He was still groggy but gave me a flicker of a smile. I sat down on a rickety chair next to him. "Everything went as well as we could expect," I began. Bit by bit, I gave him an outline of what we had found and what we'd done about it. I knew he would remember little of what I said, but perhaps he would at least retain some general sense of the operation. He gave me another faint smile when I finished my summary.

He was awake enough that I could give him a quick post-op neurologic exam. He had always had normal sensation; I wanted to verify that that was still true. Using a pin, I started poking at the middle of his chest; sensation was fine. I continued down his body. As I passed his belly button, he looked puzzled. His frown as good as said, "Why aren't you still poking me?"

Not good news. Somewhat panicky, I poked deeper and deeper with the safety pin. Little specks of blood started appearing, but nothing on Lewis's facial expression changed.

"Lewis, can you feel this?"

He shook his head.

"How about this?" I poked again in his groin.

Nothing.

As I poked down his legs on either side, it was as if I was not touching Lewis at all.

"Okay, Lewis, just wiggle your toes like you did before surgery," I said.

Nothing.

"Okay, move your toes up and down now, Lewis. Up and down. Go ahead ... move them."

Nothing.

Still groggy, Lewis frowned as he tried to decipher what I was doing and what it might mean. What was it he should be able to feel or do?

"Well, Lewis, sometimes there's this little ... little, ah ..." I didn't need to finish the sentence. Little nerve problem. Little issue with paralysis. Little side effect that meant we took away what limited mobility our patient had. Lewis hadn't expected this, and I hadn't expected it either.

I walked out of the hospital exhausted, which was natural. But I was also confused and disappointed. One aspect of this surgery was different from any I'd ever done before. I'd prayed for hundreds of patients, but I'd never relied on prayer to resolve *whether to do a surgery*. Sally and I had been so sure this was the right path! We had prayed so hard and been so certain. We had been so excited to see Lewis healed!

Now there he lay: no sensation, no strength, no future.

And I had done this to him.

The restful night's sleep I had expected never came. I tossed and turned, the events of the surgery racing through my mind. The bugs hadn't caused him to be paralyzed, I sarcastically told myself. It wasn't the heat, and it wasn't the audience, and it certainly wasn't my eager assistants. The only person touching that spinal cord yesterday had been me. But what had gone wrong? Each step of the surgery had seemed God-ordained. Finding the apex of the deformity had seemed almost like a miracle. I had never inadvertently hit the spinal cord. Lewis's body had never "jumped" on the table, which sometimes happens if the cord is traumatized. Despite the primitive conditions, everything had gone smoothly. Yet despite all that, somehow, I had paralyzed this man who believed that I was there to heal him.

Again and again I thought, *The hospital's head of surgery had been right: I should never have attempted such an ambitious operation in that hospital. Who did I think I was?*

I normally love breakfast, but after that fitful night's sleep, a cup of black coffee was all I could tolerate. I walked to the hospital in a daze. If the birds were singing, I didn't hear them. If the sun was shining, I couldn't see it.

Navigating down the crowded halls toward the orthopedic floor, I vaguely heard greetings: "Good morning, doctor!"

Doctor! I thought. *How about "butcher"? How about "clumsy oaf"? Congratulations, Scott, create a malpractice suit on your second case in Malawi!* It was no consolation to think there had never been a suit against an orthopedist here—there had never been an orthopedist in Malawi before Ed and me. And today I was really not sure I could be counted as one. I'd never had even a resident handle a case with this bad an outcome. I would probably have fired him if I had.

When I touched Lewis's forehead, I felt a bit of a fever. As I expected, the normal charting hadn't been done. I wasn't angry. How in the world could a nurse with 106 patients take the time to plot the temperature of one of them? Thirty percent of her patients at any given time probably had fever unrelated to anything orthopedic. Malaria, dysentery, and a dozen diseases I'd never seen were brought into the hospital by these patients.

"Good morning, Lewis," I began. "Did you have a good night?"

The answer was a weak smile.

"Let's do the postoperative check again." I got my trusty safety pin out and began pricking his body, trying to locate areas of sensation.

"Feel that?"

Lewis's face was blank.

"Okay, how about this?"

Once again, nothing.

"Feel anything here, Lewis?" I could see the panic in his eyes. Did he see the panic in mine?

"Okay, now down this leg—feel anything?"

I dreaded asking the next question. "Move your toes."

Not even a flicker.

Nothing had changed since the night before. Evidently the six-hour surgery that Sally and I had prayed so hard over had been an utter failure. I was grasping for straws now. Should I take him back to the OR? To do what? Make him even worse?

"Okay, Lewis, let's do something I didn't test before surgery," I said. I couldn't think of anything else to do. "I'm holding your big toe, Lewis. Am I pushing it down or up?"

"Up," he said.

I blinked. He was right. Was it just luck? After all, he had a fifty-fifty chance by guessing. "Okay, Lewis, I'm moving it again. Which way, down or up?"

"Down," he answered.

"Okay, how about now?"

"Up."

"How about now?" I could hear the excitement in my voice.

"Down."

"How about now?"

"Down, again." Now I heard a hint of excitement in his voice as well.

"How about now?"

"Still down."

"How about now?" I was nearly shouting!

"Up."

"Let's try the other leg now, Lewis. How about now?"

Down. Down. Up. Up. Up.

I stepped a half pace back from the bed and took a breath to calm myself. "Lewis, you knew exactly where your toes were at all times. What this means is, you have position sense. So your spinal cord is intact!"

He seemed pleased, but that was nothing compared to the relief flooding through me.

"It is very, very likely that you will regain your strength and sensation. You have an excellent chance of returning to work on the railroad, even of playing soccer with your boys again!"

Lewis would walk again!

And I felt like I was flying as I retraced my steps home. "Sally, Lewis will walk again!" I called as I burst through the front door. "Sally, we hadn't got it wrong! Just as it says, 'Believe that you have received it.'" I collapsed into a chair. She ran in from the kitchen, and there we were, The Team: the surgeon, the praying anchoress, and the Healer.

⤙

After a week or so of recovery, I removed Lewis's chest tube. After that, my focus on him was diluted by an onslaught of other patients. Word had gotten out! Patient after patient rolled through, most with tubercular spinal deformities like his. Thankfully, no more post-op neurologic losses!

The patients and their conditions became a blur. There were so many similar cases that I ran through my supply of chest tubes and drains, and we had to make do with urinary catheters.

For the rest of my time in Malawi, I was called to ever more distant regional hospitals and never made it back to QE2 to see Lewis. But I often thought about him.

Seven weeks after his surgery, I was back at home resuming my normal orthopedic practice. I received a letter from Ed in Malawi:

> Lewis began moving his toes a week after you went north. The smile never left his face. He even began gaining a few pounds. His wife, four daughters, and five boys began visiting him regularly; they even began talking about "football." His boss stopped by my office and I assured him that Lewis would be able to resume his duties in about another couple of months.
>
> He left the hospital yesterday. He was walking with a slight limp. He has regained normal sensation and his strength is rapidly returning.

I couldn't wait to share that news with Sally. We had prayed so hard that Lewis would be healed. And we had prayed that God would give us the assurance to do the surgery. Not the expectation, not the wish, but the *assurance*. We had believed, which was what had made the initial results so crushing. God had tested our faith—but in the end, he had honored it.

↩

Thirteen months later, I was back in Malawi, running through the usual 100-plus patients that make up an average clinic. I had my head down, completing a chart, when the next patient walked up, and I could see only his feet and legs. I looked up—and there was Lewis's smiling face!

I looked at his wound. There was still a tiny bit of drainage. His strength was normal. He was back to playing soccer with the kids.

"Lewis," I said, "I'm going to send you some First World medicine to take care of these few persistent bugs draining out of your chest. When you finish taking that, the rest of the infection will be gone, and I will probably never see you again.

"And by the way, Lewis," I said, "you're famous. An American magazine, *Guideposts*, published the story of your faith that an American surgeon would come and heal you. Millions of people in America know you now."

Lewis has very dark skin, but I thought I could see him blushing. He looked away, unsure if he should speak. Then he turned back to look me in the eye. "Oh, doctor," he began hesitantly, "I may have said that you were the one to heal me … and I am grateful that you came. But I had prayed to Jesus. And Jesus told me he would heal me. It was Jesus."

I smiled back. He was right. Prayer had given him optimism, which was so important in his healing. And then God had done the rest!

I would have given him a hug, but a *mzungu* (white person) doesn't do that in front of fifty other black Africans. After all he'd been through, I didn't want Lewis to die of embarrassment.

There's a picture of Lewis sitting in front of me as I write this, his ever-present smile beaming out at me. He sent it to me, along with his thanks for the antibiotic and his reassurance that all was well. Other than the fact that his arms hang down to his knees because his back is three vertebrae too short, he looks good in his suit and tie. It is probably the only picture Lewis ever had taken of himself.

We both learned a lot about trust, perhaps me more than Lewis. After all, he wasn't surprised to be healed, because he had prayed to Jesus. But I had prayed too, and my prayer too had been answered, though at first I had doubted it. I didn't have the depth of faith my patient had. But it's growing.

CHAPTER 11

KIPKOECK

NO PLACE I'VE BEEN HAS MORE SUPERSTITIONS AND ANXIET-
ies than Africa. Poverty is everywhere, reflected in every aspect
of the people's lives. Their homes are often huts ten to twelve feet
in diameter, in which live two adults and three or four children.
Disease is expected; in fact, many tribes won't give a baby a name
until it reaches its first birthday, which sadly many still fail to do.
The causes of illness are often still attributed to the spirit world.
Placating those spirits is a daily challenge. Understanding how to
do so is often the role of the elderly women of the village.

Chizoba was one of those women. An octogenarian, she told
time by events. Her passing blood, which should have happened
about the time she was thirteen, was the year of the big prairie
fire. She started Standard 1—which could have happened at any
age from seven to seventeen, whenever her family could afford
the school dress and a pair of shoes—the year there was nothing
to eat because of the plague of locusts. She was born the year of
the big wind from the south, which was also the time when the
Christian missionaries visited her village and her father came to
believe in the man-god called Jesus.

The rural Kenya that Chizoba grew up in is little different

from what it was five hundred years ago. There are schools now, but children back then received an informal education that might not have been very different. One big change is that children are immunized now—but in some areas, half the village children still die by age five of the diseases most villagers attribute to hostile spirits. About 125 years ago, Christian missionaries came to Kenya bringing news of the one true God, who appears as one essence and three persons. It was a confusing message, so like many rural Kenyans, Chizoba kept her charms and amulets bundled in a rag at the back of the hut, just in case. And those "cases," when they came, usually involved disease. Sometimes the causes of those diseases were understood; more often they weren't. Chizoba worried a lot about the spirits that she believed cause these diseases. They were the primary source of stress in her life.

Her village in the bush, miles from a road, which is only a dirt track anyway, has only a dozen huts built of acacia branches and roofed mostly with plastic tarps. She knows everybody; they're her sisters, daughters, nieces, and cousins.

Mama Mzazi, her niece, has a son named Kipkoeck, who was born the year of the floods. He is different. So different he's scary. As long as Chizoba can remember, he has walked funny, with his knees against each other and his feet dragging. And he couldn't stand straight up—instead, he always looked like he was getting ready to jump … but he couldn't do that either. Even when his cousins first learned to walk, usually when they still had a belly that made them look like they were going to have a baby, they could run faster than he could.

Kipkoeck's words slurred together so he couldn't say his own name. No one took time to listen to him except Chizoba. He wasn't dumb like people said; it just took time to understand his speech.

His birth, Mama Mzazi said, had required a really hard labor.

Her pains lasted for two days before he finally came out. He didn't breathe right away. Everyone thought he would die. But he surprised them and survived.

Still, he didn't begin walking when his older brothers and sisters had. He was almost three before he developed that shuffling gait, dragging his legs, struggling laboriously from hut to hut. Sometimes Kipkoeck (whose Western name is Geoffrey, but nobody calls him that) would suddenly fall to the ground, his mouth would fill with foam, his tongue would hang out, and his eyes would roll back like he was trying to see inside his own head. His arms and legs would thrash around. Even though whatever was happening to him lasted just a few minutes, it seemed as if it went on forever. Following some deep sighs, his breathing would return to normal. Then he would just lie there, sleeping. Some said that if you touched him at those times, you would die. Everyone thought he was full of evil spirits. They were afraid that some of those spirits might leave him and come into them. He was scary.

Chizoba prayed to God for him … but just to be sure, she also went to the traditional healer for some special powder to rub on his head when he foamed at the mouth.

In spite of all that, he was Chizoba's favorite. Not everyone's, though. His brothers and sisters would tease Kipkoeck and then run away. They wouldn't let him play. But Chizoba would sometimes get the rolled-up sack that was the village soccer ball and roll it to him. Since he couldn't run, he was the goalie. Mostly in those games he would just lie there, but sometimes he was able to block one of her shots. Even though Chizoba was so, so old, they were buddies. He would follow her like a puppy dog. Chizoba was his only friend.

And she began to pray more and more to Jesus that he would make Kipkoeck like all the other village children.

Because he talked slowly and was hard for other people to understand, Mama Mzazi said he wasn't smart enough to go to school. But she always knew what he was saying, and he knew that he could come to her for what he needed.

Kipkoeck's father wasn't around much. He had gone to live with a woman in a village an hour away. He was afraid of Kipkoeck. He said that his son was cursed.

Kipkoeck's seizures got worse. This, the medicine man said, was because the evil spirits were growing inside him. How could Kipkoeck have evil spirits, Mama Mzazi wondered? He was such a nice boy. But the villagers remained afraid of him—his evil spirits, they believed, could hurt or even kill people.

Chizoba prayed to Jesus for protection—for the people in the village, lest the evil spirits harm them, and for Kipkoeck, lest someone harm him to eliminate the threat of the evil spirits.

And just when things couldn't get any worse for Kipkoeck, he began to bend over even more. He would try to stand straight, but his back was growing a big hump. Mama Mzazi was frightened—this must mean that Kipkoeck had evil spirits after all, and that they were growing inside him.

His face was now flushed, and when you touched him his skin was burning hot. One day as he tried to get out of bed, he fell. His legs wouldn't work anymore. He couldn't even crawl. His fits were coming more often, and he would roll back and forth in his bed, sweaty, speaking words that made no sense. When asked what was wrong, he would just roll his eyes, and foam would come out of his mouth.

About that time, one of the villagers came upon a crocodile, massive and ancient, sunning itself in the sand not far from the river near their village. The villagers had known this crocodile for scores of years, and had named it Mamba. Chizoba's grandmother had said that even her mother had feared it. At sixteen feet, it was the prince of evil. Sometimes Mamba would crawl along the riverbed and grab one of the village women washing her clothes. It would drag her underwater and stuff her into a crevice. A week or so later, her mangled dress would float to the surface, mute evidence of her fate. Mamba was a servant of the devil, the villagers believed, and therefore it was the source of powerful magic.

But now Mamba was approaching its hundredth year; it had lost some teeth, and a new mamba had claimed this most choice part of the river. But as the old crocodile lay in the sun to die, it still possessed its mystic power, and Mzazi's brothers surrounded it and began a centuries-old ritual of taking its malevolent power. Using his razor-sharp assegai, one man would feign a stab at its chest, then plunge his knife into its leg. When the crocodile whipped its tail at one of them, a man opposite would pierce his exposed underbelly. The struggle went on and on. Suddenly Mamba's vicious tail shattered one of the younger men's tibia. The cracking sound was heard even in the village a quarter mile away. His older brother ran toward the croc, lifting his assegai over his head and screaming his tribe's ancient war chant. He brought the point of his assegai into that golf-ball-sized spot just behind those demonic eyes. The croc's tail slashed right and left, pounding an adjacent mopane tree. But its movements gradually slowed until they no longer had the lethal force that had so easily snapped the young man's tibia.

Exhausted, the men stepped back and marveled at the strength of this reptile they both honored and feared. They knew it would continue to move for a few hours. They would need five more men from the village to help carry it. It weighed, after all, nearly a quarter of a ton. Some of the men would refuse to help, afraid of the beast's mystical power. They had said prayers to the croc's ancestors many times. Would those ancestors now take revenge? It would be necessary to appease their anger.

Leery of that still slowly twisting tail, with shaking hands, the men rolled the croc over. They removed its stomach and intestines, site of some of Mamba's strongest magical powers. When they cut open its stomach, they found the remains of a faded blue T-shirt. They had heard that a fisherman upstream had gone missing a few weeks before. Now his widow could begin her mourning. They would give her some of the tail meat so she could appease the spirits.

Still Mamba's tail continued moving, menacingly, rhythmically back and forth. There would be a sudden, vicious lash that would send the men scampering away—then it would go back to moving slowly back and forth.

With a sense of reverence for Mamba's power and importance, the men continued the autopsy, cutting free the sack adjacent to the creature's liver. This held the most powerful of all its malicious spirits. Only the eldest of the men was willing to touch it, and he shuddered as he placed it in the pouch they'd fashioned from an old cow that had died a few months before.

Still, even with the reptile's belly cut open and many of its organs removed, the croc's tail moved in slow, mesmerizing circles. This was a death in slow motion, which confirmed Mamba's malevolent power. The underworld of this majestic killer would now be furious and would insist on retribution, on lethal vengeance against those who killed Mamba and on their whole village as well.

So that evening, the men covered themselves with the

belly fat of the croc, sang songs, and said prayers to the spirit of Mamba, then dug shallow graves and buried themselves in the sand, circumvallating the village to appease the spirit world, using their own witchcraft and the power they had appropriated from Mamba to ward off the marauding hyenas.

By morning, Mamba's tail had stopped moving. It was now safe to bring the carcass into the village.

But there was more to be done to appease the spirits offended by their killing of this creature. Their local witch doctor did not have power enough, so they hired another who, after eating parts of a corpse—yes, parts of a human body dug from a shallow grave near the village—made an especially strong curse to protect the village. Then he imparted that curse to a *mushongo* (a dead chicken now carrying the deadly curse) and cast it into the river.

Then, using his own bag of amulets, dead bones, and specially prepared powders, he made an especially powerful potion for each villager to consume. It produced uncontrolled vomiting, but that only served to convince the villagers that the potion was indeed powerful and that it had saved the village. Surely many would have died without the witch doctor's strong potions!

This belief in the power of evil is a powerful and unavoidable part of Africa. For Chizoba, Mzazi, and Kipkoeck, Satan has a face. He is not merely a religious abstraction. Evil is personified by witch doctors, and its consequences are boldly displayed.

But if witch doctors are dreaded, medical doctors are venerated. Much of sub-Saharan Africa was converted to Christianity by medical missionaries. Nowhere is the contrast between Satan and Christ as stark. Witch doctors can bring sickness, even death, if they are paid by an angry villager seeking revenge. Medical doctors bring relief from the scourges still killing far too many.

The death of the crocodile complicated things for Kipkoeck.

Mama Mzazi was sure that the crocodile had brought more demons, and that those demons had taken control of her Kipkoeck—how else to explain his new weakness, fever, and inability even to crawl or speak? Other villagers shared their fears that next these spirits would be jumping from Kipkoeck to her, then to her other children, even to Kipkoeck's cousins. No one in the village wanted to become like him, so they were afraid even to go where he was in his newly weakened state, now curled pathetically on the floor in a corner of the hut. His older brothers knew what they had to do: To save the village from the demons, they had to get rid of Kipkoeck.

He was easily picked up and carried, his body having withered so much. They took him out into the bush and tried one more time to cast out his evil spirits, but he kept shaking, his eyes rolling back in his head, foam coming from his mouth. So they put him under a tree sacred to the village and left him.

When they came back to the village, and Mama Mzazi and Chizoba saw that Kipkoeck was no longer with them, they were afraid for him. They knew that by morning he wouldn't be under that tree anymore. His smell would bring the hyenas during the night. Mama Mzazi prayed that he would be unconscious when the hyenas came, but if not, that he would die quickly. Everyone knew that hyenas start to eat their prey before it is dead.

Mama Chizoba prayed that Jesus wouldn't let the hyenas kill him at all. Maybe Jesus had a better plan. So she put on her shawl and set out on her own, carrying a blanket under her arm. "It's not right!" she said. She motioned to her oldest nephew to follow.

They were gone for two days. When she came back to the village, she told everyone that they had taken Kipkoeck to the white doctor's hospital. She was not sure that the hospital would take Kipkoeck, but because they knew Jesus, maybe they would.

And they did!

She had not told the white doctors that Kipkoeck was possessed by evil spirits. Maybe their Jesus was stronger. And when they saw how nice Kipkoeck was, how could they think he was evil?

Before she crawled onto her mat to sleep that night, Mama Chizoba prayed to Jesus one more time that these Christian doctors would help.

↪

She was right; we would at least try.

I had just gotten off the plane from London, the second leg of my flight to Kenya. Two hours later, I met Geoffrey Kipkoeck on my rounds. The smell he gave off as I approached his hospital bed said much about the seriousness of his condition. Our young African intern concluded his litany of Kipkoeck's dire illnesses by mumbling that he would soon be dead.

Kipkoeck was suffering intermittent status epilepticus, a very serious condition in which the brain locks into a prolonged seizure. His seizures would last for three or four minutes, then resume after a brief pause. The cycle occurred over and over again. The seizures interfered even with his breathing; that alone might be fatal

The characteristic spastic motions with his arms indicated cerebral palsy.

The hump on his back was not a mass; it was the bones of his twisted spinal column, a curvature that had come about from the collapse of his thoracic vertebrae, caused by the tuberculosis he'd had when he was just five years old. The medicine they'd given him then had killed the bacilli in his lungs, but they hadn't continued his medicine long enough to get to the bacteria sequestered in his bones. So, inexorably, the *Mycobacterium tuberculosis* had eaten away his spinal vertebrae, causing them to crumble like a rotten tree, crushing his spinal cord. This deformity had also contracted his lung capacity.

Kipkoeck was only eleven years old.

I walked away from his bed doubtful that, no matter what we did, he would still be alive the next morning. To take him into the OR first thing the next morning, in his dehydrated state (he'd had no water for the past thirty-six hours), with a fever of 104 and uncontrollable incontinence, felt like an execution. But to do nothing would be worse. We had to at least make the effort, however desperate and futile it seemed.

We started an IV loaded with antibiotics for the secondary infections of who knows what. There were sure to be plenty. Treatment of his tuberculosis would require nine months, if he lived that long.

I ordered a couple of units of blood, although I doubted that even a healthy patient could survive all the procedures that would be required to put this young man on the road to health. More likely, his status epilepticus, his paraplegia, his tuberculosis, his urinary tract infection, and his septicemia (blood poisoning) would kill him that night before we could even operate. And if not, his surgeon's inadequacies could kill him in the morning.

To the list of medications and procedures we added one more, the one we never left out: prayer. I prayed for Kipkoeck that evening, and later in the night when I awoke worrying about the surgery, and again at breakfast. There would be one more prayer, at surgery, just before we made the incision.

When I saw Kipkoeck the next morning, I marveled at his endurance. His seizures were now continuous. At least the anesthetic would mercifully, albeit temporarily, stop his status epilepticus. Also, if the pus could be drained from the abscess around his spine, it should resolve his fever.

Surgeons are natural optimists. You can't begin operations day in and day out expecting to fail. If you do, you don't last very long. Neither do your patients. Operating on spinal abscesses resulting from tuberculosis had become one of the operations I did most often in Africa. So, beginning at the center of the back, at the eighth thoracic spinous process, the scalpel traced diagonally along the rib to the front of the chest. Kipkoeck's abscess was so large that I needed to take the diaphragm down, so we curved the incision across his abdomen downward toward his umbilicus.

Once I opened his chest and collapsed his lung, the oblong sac of pus bulged into view. Then it slipped beneath the dome of his diaphragm. To uncover it, we had to open his abdomen by cutting into his diaphragm as well. It always amazed me that even a healthy child could tolerate this drastic surgery. We had nearly cut Kipkoeck in two. It was a miracle that he had survived to this point.

We removed the eighth and ninth ribs; we would later fashion them into bone struts to replace the destroyed vertebrae. Then I made a small incision in the infected mass, and the slurping of the suction began to decompress the abscess—something that always feels perversely good to me!

When I'd made the incisions that exposed the back side of his spinal abscess, the destruction revealed was appalling. His once solid column of bone now looked like road gravel, and I knew that each bony pebble was impregnated with millions of tuberculous bacilli. They would be useless as bone graft material.

Curetting and chiseling out the dead bone eventually revealed the spinal cord. A large fragment of a collapsed vertebra was flattening the apex of his spinal cord. I removed it, allowing the ribbon-like cord to immediately expand—but the persistent crease indicated that this obstruction had been there a long time. If Kipkoeck survived, Mother Nature would expand and partially reshape his spinal cord over the next few years. With a little bit of luck and a lot of prayer, there was a chance that he would regain his ability to walk, albeit still with his scissoring cerebral palsy gait.

But for that to happen, he would first have to survive.

With the source of the fever removed, the status epilepticus (almost continuous seizures) should resolve. Increasing his anticonvulsive therapy should completely resolve that problem.

Now, from the two ribs we'd removed, we fashioned a series of tiny barrel staves to bridge the gap left by the tuberculous abscess. Because of his young age, Kipkoeck's ability to regenerate bone would be excellent.

We'd been at this for three and a half hours, but my young patient was hanging in there. So were we. We biopsied a couple of lymph nodes along the spine to determine the possible extent of his tuberculosis, then began sewing his diaphragm back together. An hour and a half later, his chest was closed, and the tube allowing for further drainage and full expansion of his lungs was securely in place. The anesthetist nodded to indicate that, amazingly, the patient had remained stable.

More amazingly, so had I. A quiet "Thank you, Lord" concluded the procedure.

∽

There is no place on the medical chart to explain how or why this patient did so well. There are sites to record blood pressure, medications, pulse rate, and other vital signs. What is absent is a record of the prayers offered for this young man by Sally, by some of his extended family, and by our prayer partners back in the States.

His recovery was amazing. His fever stayed down, and his seizures first came under control and finally ceased altogether. He began eating like a typical eleven-year-old, and an amber glow replaced the burgundy blush of his face.

The only person more pleased than I was Mama Chizoba, who had returned the day after surgery. She had no money to pay for even the most modest accommodation. How she found food I don't know. I guess our hospital fed her as well. She stayed the course, always at Kipkoeck's bedside, her toothless smile lighting up the ward.

Four weeks after surgery, with a body cast and packets of medication, Geoffrey Kipkoeck and Mama Chizoba returned to their village.

There were at first hushed whispers. "It is the ghost of Kipkoeck come back to haunt us!"

Remembering the skeleton they had abandoned under a tree, incontinent, convulsing, and apparently doomed to the hyenas, his extended family barely recognized him; he was already putting on weight, and his skin had an earthy glow.

As they cautiously drew near him, there was nervous laughter. If this was really him, he looked better than they'd ever seen him. Still ... might it just be an apparition? His cousin poked a finger at his side to see if would slice through this phantom. Kipkoeck jumped ... and his cousin jumped even higher!

A few weeks later, his sister was the first to notice that he was able to wiggle his big toe. Within another week, all five toes were moving, as was his ankle.

With a few tree boughs arranged as a makeshift porch beside the front door, he was able sit in the African sun and feel its warmth. He began to reintegrate into the village, and the people gradually lost their fear of him. He held court. People who previously refused to come near him for fear of catching his evil spirits could see that those were no longer part of him. They now drew close and touched him—but cautiously, since they still weren't sure whether he might not be a ghoul.

Or—was it possible that he might now have a power greater than that of the evil spirits? His eyes no longer rolled uncontrollably, and foam no longer spewed from his mouth. Instead, for the first time in his eleven years, he smiled.

Gradually, he became a full member of the village community, treated no differently than his brothers and sisters and cousins.

∽

A little over a year later, in the midst of another busy clinic, the endless parade of disabled children was interrupted by the appearance of a child who appeared normal and healthy. His smile cheered the dimly lit room. I had no idea who he was, but he seemed to know me. He was accompanied by an attentive man who kept nodding his head eagerly. If anything, his smile was bigger than that of the boy who apparently was his son.

When the interpreter said, "This is Kipkoeck," it was as if he was announcing the Pope!

Kipkoeck walked with only the slightest shuffle. His spine, still not completely straight, was camouflaged by a loose-fitting shirt, his telltale hump barely visible. It would be with him the rest of his life.

Through an interpreter, his father whispered that he no

longer needed to leave the village to see other women. He wanted to be with his son. "His spirit can bring people back from the dead," he said.

I noticed one other person.

Standing deferentially to the rear was the wizened Mama Chizoba, smiling her toothless grin, head bobbing knowingly. Was that a prayer she was mouthing? If it was, it was a *thank you*—not to me, the white doctor, but to the One who had healed Kipkoeck.

CHAPTER 12

Miss Modesty and the Arrival of AIDS

When the young woman entered my examining room in Malawi, she shuffled, nearly falling, with an awkward, lurching gait, dragging her left leg. She gasped for breath, gulping a mouthful of air at a time. Her head was bowed, her eyes exploring the dirty floor. That posture suggested timidity, but her face, what I could see of it, signaled something more. I saw shame. Perhaps that explained why she was alone.

I guessed her to be about thirteen, maybe as old as fifteen. Her clothes, if you could call the rags that hung from her shoulders by that name, suggested she might be even older. I knew from past experience that she wouldn't know her age, so there was no point in asking. It would just embarrass her more. Perhaps she was older, as her exposed breasts suggested she'd passed through puberty.

I motioned for her to climb onto the examining table. As she did, she grimaced in pain. The pain appeared to come from her left hip, flexed about thirty degrees so that her left leg scissored across her right leg. Not only was she in pain, she shrank from me as if she were expecting a beating.

"How long have you been hurting?" I asked through an interpreter.

She shook her head and mumbled that she wasn't sure. It had been a long time, she said. A season ago, the village healer had rubbed a potion on it, but it kept getting worse. So the healer had told her that she must be very bad for the gods to bring her this suffering.

It was then that I noticed the tattered X-ray she held. Staring at her feet, she offered the frayed folder that would verify her condition and confirm her shame.

It was no wonder that health care in Malawi cost only three cents on the dollar. Most patients entered the hospital with diseases so advanced that I rarely needed to order expensive tests. In this case, there would be no reason to order the MRI or CT scans, let alone the blood work that would be routine in the States.

I turned to the young doctors-in-training with me and explained, "This young lady has a classic septic hip." I hung up the X-ray on the view box so everyone could see. "The infection has been going on for a long time and has destroyed the joint."

The X-ray provided a single view of her pelvis. Her right hip was normal, and the development of the bone indicated that she was in her late teens, her growth plates nearly closed. The left hip joint was severely damaged, and the accumulation of pus from the infection had pushed the femoral head out of its socket.

After a short lecture on septic joints, I told my assistants, "All that's necessary now is to confirm that she has no tenderness in her other joints and schedule her for surgery."

As I attempted to pull back her garment to evaluate her right hip, her hands grabbed mine, preventing me from raising her skirt. She shook her head firmly. Clearly she was not about to expose any part of her groin region to this total stranger—especially one who was white.

"It doesn't matter," I said to the interns. "Let's respect her modesty. Schedule her for a debridement (removal of dead tissue) and possible hip fusion tomorrow. I'm leaving in a couple of days, but you'll be able to handle the rest of her care."

The debridement would remove the dead bone that had been destroyed by the infection. Fusion in her case would require three or four long screws placed through the femoral neck and head and then, with the femoral head returned to its correct anatomic place, the socket of the pelvis. New bone eventually forms a bridge, making the pelvic and femoral bone one. Amazingly, after surgery, the patients usually walk with a barely perceptible limp and, most importantly, have no pain.

The next day, after three or four routine (at least for Malawi) surgical procedures on other patients, we brought "Miss Modesty" into the OR. As the preoperative sedation took hold, I was finally able to remove her hands from in front of her "private parts," as she referred to them, and examine her hip. Her inguinal lymph nodes, at the edge of her stained underpants, were not only swollen, as I had expected, but were draining copious amounts of pus. Those nodes, loaded with white blood cells designed to trap the bacteria, had been overwhelmed by the virulence of her microbial invaders, spreading her infection by bursting through the overlying skin. *Stoic* hardly describes her pain tolerance—she had fatalistically endured months of excruciating pain, not to mention the noxious odor. That, she couldn't hide.

"Attempting to do a fusion in this active infection is taking an unnecessary risk," I said to the young physician who would be assisting in the surgery. "We need to drain this and remove the dead and infected bone. It also looks like we'll need to have vaginal cultures done, since our patient also has a foul-smelling vaginal discharge. But it's probably the same organisms."

I shook my head. "Sadly, it turns out that our little Miss Modesty is already well into her professional career. I hope she was well paid by whoever gave her this infection. We'll go ahead and treat her for gonorrhea because it's so widespread, and add broad-spectrum antibiotic coverage to include various other pathogens that could be mixed in. I doubt this mess came from a single customer."

⌒

It had been her mother, I later found out, who had brought the men to their hut. The young girl had lain there as her mother demanded. At first it had hurt, and she had bled as she had been doing monthly since the last harvest. But as more and more men came, it didn't hurt anymore. And her younger brothers now had food to eat.

But her grandmother had accused her of being wicked. "How else can we explain this terrible sickness that twists and coils your leg?"

The girl believed that her grandmother and the village healer, the one who had told her that she must be very bad for the gods to have given her this pain, must be right, but the stress of her humiliation was exceeded by her pain.

And now that her disfigurement was obvious, the men no longer came.

Her modesty had already been violated by many men before she arrived at our hospital. She covered herself now out of shame—out of her desperate desire that no one else see the damage visited upon her by those who had exploited her sexually, with no regard for her welfare.

‍⌒

The next day on rounds I told the local doctor, "Take the drains out when the pus clears. We need to schedule her surgery for when I come back. By then this infection should be cleaned up and we can proceed with the hip fusion."

The next day I flew on to South Africa. I was leafing through the newspaper at what was then Jan Smuts Airport in Johannesburg when an article caught my eye. The first public health survey on a new disease called acquired immune deficiency syndrome, or AIDS, had found that Malawi had less than a 3 percent incidence even in the high-risk population—people like my patient Miss Modesty. The reporter pointed out that this rate of infection was much lower than in South Africa, where 20 to 30 percent of the young female population was infected with AIDS. I found the Malawian statistic encouraging, since Malawi at that point didn't have adequate diagnostic testing. Then I moved on to the next article and thought nothing more about it. It was 1986. AIDS had been in Africa for eight or nine decades, but until urbanization occurred, it had remained a silent biological time bomb.

Two months later, I was back in Malawi, and Miss Modesty had been readmitted to the hospital, ready for her hip fusion— and in much less pain, now that the infection had been eradicated.

Once she was asleep, we could see that the scars where the inguinal lymph nodes had spontaneously ruptured and drained were now healed, indicating that the antibiotics and removal of dead tissue had done their job. She now had a 40-degree hip flexion contracture, with about 15 degrees of fixed adduction as well—in other words, at rest, her hip was bent over her good leg and turned inward so she was "pigeon-toed."

"This is going to be a difficult fusion," I told my new assistants. "The anatomy will be distorted, and given the infection she fought for so long, we can't be sure what amount of damage we'll find. She also seems to have lost a fair amount of weight since I last saw her. That's a surprise, since her infection has been under control."

I didn't add the rest of what I was thinking: *And I've also been praying for this woman, because we don't see disease this advanced in Harrisburg, Pennsylvania.*

Sadly, because of the absence of adequate medical facilities and doctors, I had become proficient in hip fusions during my prior trips to Africa. An operation that an orthopedist might perform once in a decade in America I would do once or twice a week in Africa. The scarcity of antibiotics allows hip infections to become explosively destructive, and the unavailability and expense of prosthetic hip replacements leaves no other choice.

"Fortunately," I told my assistants as we worked, "a successful hip fusion results in minimal gait changes and, as opposed to total hip replacement, is guaranteed to last a lifetime."

The surgery progressed normally. A significant portion of the acetabulum (the socket into which the head of the femur fits) had been destroyed by the infection, distorting the girl's anatomy, as I had suspected. I found myself working blindly from the back side of the pelvis, thinking how unusual that was, except of course in Africa. Orthopedists have their normal routes and landmarks as they navigate the human body; it's just another kind of geography. But it was disconcerting to find many of my normal landmarks missing.

"Before we attempt the fusion," I said, "it's mandatory that we make sure we've gotten any remaining dead tissue out that we may have left from the first surgery. Things were so distorted then that it's more than likely we left behind some dead bone, and with no blood supply, those fragments are a storehouse of bacteria. Since these areas are by definition avascular, the antibiotics, which travel through the bloodstream, have no way to reach them. So, the bacteria flourish."

Illustrating my point, I began pulling out chunks of distorted bone.

I noticed a few drops of my perspiration landing on the surgical drapes. *Will I ever get comfortable doing this kind of surgery?* I asked myself. *And ... was that a tremor in my right hand?*

I was just about finished when I noticed a recessed cavity in her ilium, her main pelvic bone, created by her prior abscess. Tucked behind her pelvis, in the depths of our operative site, was a ragged chunk of dead bone. I pulled on it. It seemed to be caught by some adjacent tissue. I tugged harder. And again, harder. That time, the jagged piece of bone came free.

It also tore my surgical glove, dousing my index finger in her blood.

But at the moment, that was a minor concern compared with the torrent of blood pouring from the cavity from which I'd just removed the bone fragment. There must have been an artery, now ruptured, attached by scar tissue to the bone I'd removed. The torn artery was instantly hidden by an expanding pool of blood that overwhelmed our primitive suction.

"The tear of this artery probably didn't transect it completely," I said to my wide-eyed assistants, aware that my voice had risen along with my anxiety. "If the artery was transected, it would retract and go into spasm. The arterial smooth muscles wrapped around the torn artery would contract and pinch off and control the bleeding. She'd have been better off if the artery had been transected. Since the artery can't constrict itself, she could bleed out."

I looked up at the anesthesia nurse. "This patient's blood pressure may begin drop—"

"Did you hit a gusher?" she interrupted. "Her pressure's in free fall!"

Finding the source of the bleeding was like groping for a ghost in a dark room. As the pelvic cavity continued to fill with blood, I could find no place to use a hemostat, the clamp we usually use to close off blood vessels. Our patient was in grave danger, and I was desperate. I could see nothing, but if I didn't find the artery and somehow halt the flow of blood, Modesty would die on the operating table.

Reaching into the crimson pool, searching blindly, I felt around for a pulse, any pulse. At last I was able to sense a faint pulse and grasp the tear of the artery between my thumb and index finger, and the flow of blood slowed to a trickle.

My pulse is probably just as faint as hers is, I thought.

"If the artery retracts into the recesses of the pelvis, I'll never find it again," I warned my assistants. "Finding the torn blood vessel once was a miracle, and you don't get a second chance at that.

"Gentlemen," I continued. "I'm about to teach you something that you don't often see in textbooks but that I learned in Vietnam. We might be able to control the blood flow and get hemostasis by simple compression. But we have to maintain the compression for at least ten minutes to allow the blood to clot and seal the arterial laceration. That's going to seem like an eternity, so it's important to measure the time by a clock." Without looking up, I added, "So, what's that wall clock say? Tell me when ten minutes has gone by."

With an enthusiasm intended to mask my own anxiety, I launched into an impromptu lecture on anatomy, osteomyelitis, and the treatment of septic joints. Soon we were involved in an intense professor-student dialogue. I was glad I'd mentioned the ten-minute time frame, because we got so engrossed in a question-and-answer period that none of us thought of the time.

Finally my cramping fingers prompted me to ask, "What time is it, anyway?"

Looking over his shoulder, the resident who had initially checked the wall clock answered sheepishly, "It is still ten minutes after two o'clock, same as it was when I first looked."

I shook my head in frustration. Why would I think the wall clock would work when the suction didn't work, the OR instruments often didn't work, and frankly, it didn't seem I was working very well either? The resident had nothing to be embarrassed about—it was a case of all-round malfunction. But we still had to save Miss Modesty's life.

"Okay, we'll wait another five minutes," I said. "And to be on the safe side, we'll use the anesthetist's wristwatch to time it." That extra five minutes, ticking from the tiny Timex on the anesthetist's wrist, seemed like another half hour.

"We're counting on coagulation to clot the blood flow," I reminded the group as we waited. "And her low blood pressure from blood loss will coincidentally lessen the force on the clot, diminishing the chance that it will be washed away. Have the suction ready. I will slowly take my fingers off the artery, and we will pray that Mother Nature has done what you and I couldn't do: stop her bleeding."

I was waiting for the awkward question, "What do we do if it doesn't work?" But fortunately no one asked that, because in this OR—in this country—I simply didn't have an answer.

I gently released the tension on my thumb and index finger, which were numb by then. Three pairs of eyes focused on the depths of the wound, waiting for the blood to gurgle up, fill the cavity, and possibly end Modesty's life.

A few seconds went by ... nothing.

Fifteen seconds ... still no sign of blood.

Thirty seconds, the same.

When we counted past a minute, I could exhale and say confidently, "We've got hemostasis."

I removed my hand from the cavity and inspected my ripped glove. My thumb and index finger were now both drenched in blood. Reusing gloves for reasons of economy has its drawbacks.

And to make it worse, Miss Modesty wasn't the only one hemorrhaging that morning. Earlier, a paring knife had slipped in my wet hand as I was dicing fruit for my breakfast cereal. The laceration was deep, but I had been in a hurry, so after I sucked on it and applied the requisite ten minutes of pressure, the bleeding had stopped. In the States I would have canceled the day's surgery—that cut on my finger would have made it impossible to truly sterilize my hands with a pre-op scrub, since once the skin isn't intact, bacteria embedded in the wound stubbornly refuse to be sterilized. But that wasn't an option in Malawi, where I had dozens and dozens of patients waiting for surgery and a limited amount of time.

My fresh laceration had bathed in Miss Modesty's blood for about fifteen minutes. But this wasn't the time to contemplate how our mishap might have affected me. "Let's close this wound, put in some drains, and cast the hip so that as it stiffens, it will be in a functional position. It's possible that, with this amount of bone destruction, a spontaneous fusion will occur as part of the healing process. If it does, we'll have saved her another operation."

As we closed her wound I reflected on my young patient. I now knew more about her than she had wanted to reveal. It was obvious how she was helping to put food on the family table. She was a breadwinning prostitute. Her deep shame told me that even helping her family survive wasn't motivation enough to overcome her reluctance to submit to and experience that violation.

And now, I thought ironically, *I'm her blood brother.* Thankfully, the incidence of AIDS was only 3 percent in Malawi, even in her high-risk category. One chance in thirty-three. Not too bad.

A few months later, in another airport lounge someplace else in the world, I happened upon another article concerning AIDS in Africa. Apparently that survey I'd read in the South African newspaper had been significantly flawed. A better estimate was that the incidence of AIDS in Malawi was at least 30 percent in the sexually active teen population. Within the prostitute community, that number was estimated to be three times higher ... 90 percent.

Nine chances in ten that I had been exposed.

Was Miss Modesty a modern-day "Typhoid Mary" (one of millions), unknowingly spreading her fatal disease? I had spent more than enough time with my open cut bathed in her blood to contract this fatal infection from her.

The prevailing wisdom, in those early days of HIV, was that it required eight to twelve weeks to be certain that an AIDS exposure had resulted in infection. Praying about it now seemed to be an after-the-fact type of prayer—in essence, I would be praying for healing, not prevention. I had been, it would seem, naively underestimating my potential risk of contracting HIV. But then, in the 1980s, the epidemic was just being defined, and there was much that we still didn't know.

Still, I prayed. I prayed that I would be able to accept AIDS when the diagnosis was confirmed, and that drugs, just beginning to become available, might control my disease, although the drugs in use at the time didn't seem to work very well. AIDS was still a death sentence!

I lived with that uncertainty for seven or eight weeks, long enough to make the test for AIDS accurate, and then I couldn't stand the suspense any longer; I either had AIDs or I didn't. So one morning between surgeries (I was back in the States by that time), I rushed down to the lab. "Will someone draw some blood from me? I need to have ... to have a test for HIV ... or AIDS ... whatever. You do that test, right?" By the time I'd finished explaining, I was nearly shouting.

My shouting was met by a deathly silence. The hum of background conversation stopped. All eyes turned to me. I jumped up on the exam table and rolled up my sleeve.

Afterward, I rushed back upstairs and stood at the scrub sink preparing for my next surgery. I had just announced, I realized, to the entire population of the hospital (and soon the city of Harrisburg) that I was either gay or a regular visitor to the red-light district. Did I have a secret life they didn't know about? Well, it was too late to try to explain.

Waiting for the test results was agonizing. My life wasn't the only one at stake: If I had it, had I already passed the infection to Sally?

Two days later, I stopped at the lab secretary's desk, hoping I looked relaxed—relaxed, that is, for someone wondering whether he is about to hear a death sentence. "Do you have the results yet of that blood test I had drawn a couple days ago?" I asked. My voice sounded squeaky even to me.

Blushing, the secretary avoided my eye and muttered, "I think I can find it ... yes, here it is." She handed an envelope to me. Back then, mine had probably been the only HIV test of the week, or even the month. Anything but routine.

"Thanks so much," I said, trying to sound carefree.

I walked down the hall wondering: Where do you go to read the verdict on whether you are going to die in the next few months? The parking lot? Or should I just wait until the end of the day? Should I have someone else read it and tell me what it says?

My hands, surprisingly, weren't shaking. I think I had passed through that phase sometime earlier.

Rrrrrrip!

And there it was, staring back at me:

HIV on the left side of the paper ...

NEG on the right.

I stared at the paper for a long time, uncomprehending. How could that be? My freshly cut finger had been bathed in her blood for fifteen minutes ... and how could it be that she wasn't infected herself, given her situation?

Was it a miracle?

Was I just lucky?

⤳

A few weeks later, I spoke at church about my most recent trip to Malawi. I now felt free to tell the story of Miss Modesty and her infected hip, albeit without the mention of possible AIDS. When

I finished, a handful of people approached me to discuss Third World orthopedics and the problems of health care in Africa.

As I spoke to the others, off to the side was a man I'd known slightly for years. He was a reserved, private man. When everyone else left, he came closer and quietly said, "Was that clock you mentioned on a brownish-orange wall?" He paused. "Was it tilted, so that the twelve was rotated to where the one usually is? And did it have a white face with big black numbers?"

I had to think back to that operating room in the Queen Elizabeth Hospital in Malawi. But my memory of it was vivid—yep, the walls were a faded brown with an orange tint; the face of the clock was white, and strangely, the numbers *were* slightly tilted.

"How did you know?" I asked, somewhat taken back.

"Well, I was right in the middle of teaching my eighth-grade science class when I had this overwhelming urge—not really an urge, it was more like a command—to pray for you. I thought, *Okay, I'll wait until the class is over and then go to the teacher's lounge and pray for Scott.* But the sense of urgency was so overwhelming that I called the principal and asked him to send someone to my classroom.

"When the substitute arrived, I hurried to the lounge. When I began praying for you, I saw very clearly that catawampus clock, the brownish-orange background, and even the time—it was a little after two. And so I prayed for you. I prayed for your protection. I didn't know what protection you needed, but that didn't seem to matter. And although I prayed and prayed, for who knows how long, I noticed that the hands on the clock never moved. But now it makes sense."

So it did.

A caring God, a loving God, would take that prayer and do more with it than just protect a visiting surgeon. Since he is timeless—meaning that he saw my need and heard that man's prayer before either had happened—might he not also have answered that prayer to protect the doctor by *first* protecting a modest, frightened young girl?

Perhaps he saved the doctor by first shielding his patient. She may have been in the 10 percent free of HIV.

It would be so like him!

CHAPTER 13

FACE-TO-FACE WITH
MY OWN MORTALITY

CURE INTERNATIONAL'S FIRST HOSPITAL WAS IN KIJABE, Kenya. Their signature mountain that Sally looked on as she prayed for guidance, Mt. Longonot, rises 8,500 feet. The remnant of an extinct volcano, it's a couple miles away, in the middle of the Rift Valley. Its crater is the graveyard of a few small planes that got too close. The mountain is populated by cantankerous Cape buffalo, the occasional leopard looking for a meal, and during the dry season, elephants. Each evening the crater is highlighted by an African sunset, a kaleidoscope of eye-candy colors that closes the day.

It also routinely seduces short-term visitors to the hospital. So when Drs. Bill and Judy Baxter and their two teenage sons came to Kijabe, it was just a matter of time before they asked, showing off their few words of Maasai, "Can we climb *oloonong ot?*"

I volunteered to make the climb with them. Even though it's not a difficult climb, I didn't want them to go without an escort familiar with the mountain—the fact that it is relatively safe is what makes it dangerous. Those herds of buffalo are like the good old boys from the hills of West Virginia—they don't like strangers, making it all the more attractive to a couple of teenage boys!

We started the climb with the five of us close together, but boys on a Sunday afternoon hike are high energy, whereas us forty- and sixty-somethings, after a week of slaving in ORs, wanted a leisurely day of rest. It didn't take long for the boys to be a few hundred yards ahead of us. I remembered that a staff member had mentioned a leopard sighting recently and hurried to catch up.

Four to five hundred yards from the summit, I began experiencing pain along the left side of my neck. Like many physicians, I routinely saw myself as the first patient of the day. So without X-rays and with nothing in my medical history that suggested it, I diagnosed spondylosis (a form of degenerative arthritis) of my cervical vertebrae. A perfect illustration of the saying, "The doctor who treats himself has a fool for a patient and a knave for a doctor."

As the boys neared the summit, I thought my pain might be subsiding a bit. Having shortened the separation to about fifty yards, I slowed down because they hadn't seen that crotchety old bachelor buffalo bull in the mopane trees upwind of us, nor vice versa. I'd taken care of too many Kenyans gored and stamped on by *peaceful* buffalo. Introducing teenage boys to buffalo is best done from the bed of a four-wheel-drive vehicle, not on foot at the top of a mountain. We'd got lucky—myopic, deaf, and arthritic, he chose to ignore us.

Am I getting too old for this? I wondered.

We descended, spent but happy. I made a mental note to check with a real doctor when I got back to the States. I knew, after all, that orthopedists shouldn't moonlight as internal medical diagnosticians, and that a diagnosis of atypical angina (chest pain) is best made by a cardiologist. Still, I vaguely remembered that left-sided cervical pain was the only symptom my mother had prior to her five-vessel cardiac bypass.

Back in the States a few weeks later, Felix, a good friend who doubled as my prayer partner, Bible study partner, and sometimes cardiologist, had me on an X-ray table and was injecting radio-opaque dye into my cardiac arteries. He had positioned me so that I could watch in real time as the dye entered my heart. We were chirping along, comparing notes on our children and on Bible verses we were currently memorizing when I noticed that he'd dropped out of the conversation.

A quick anatomy lesson: Two main arteries supply blood to the heart. They branch out into smaller and ever-smaller blood vessels. Often, it is those small vessels that are partially occluded (clogged), resulting in patients proudly announcing after surgery that they were in such terrible shape they needed four or five bypasses. In fact, it is the other way around: if you are in need of only two bypasses, but those two are the main arteries in your heart, your first symptom of coronary heart disease will likely be sudden death.

The now-silent Felix injected another bolus of dye. Now I could see clearly the image of my stenotic (narrowed) arteries. "Am I right?" I said quietly. "It looks as if both arteries are blocked, nearly completely. It must be really bad when an orthopedist can make the diagnosis."

On the monitor, the left artery showed only a thin line of dye, the right marginally less. Both main arteries were nearly completely blocked. We studied the image in numb silence.

A few minutes later, the study was complete. Felix didn't mince words. "You're staying in the hospital over the weekend, and we'll make sure we get you on first thing Monday morning for bypass surgery. It's your two main arteries—one is about 95 percent occluded and the other about 85 percent. Those mild symptoms you described were misleading. If the condition were left untreated, a few months from now you could easily drop dead. And it would probably happen during one of those long spine operations you're always doing."

My kind of doc—tells it like it is.

A few hours later I was meeting with my cardiac surgeon. "This should be routine. I don't expect you'll even need blood," he said. "A few months ago, I reviewed my last 450 cases with large vessel occlusion, like yours, for a paper I presented. None of them needed transfusion. The paper will be published early next year."

That was reassuring.

I had a history with this young surgeon. While I was a clinical professor at Penn State's Medical School, he had rotated onto my service as a general surgery resident before his cardiac training. He was sharp, even though he thought of orthopedics as blunt trauma administered by brutish surgeons. He was also an occasional golfing buddy who needed to give me two a side. He could also write his name with either his right hand or his left—and either way, it was identical.

I'm not sure how any of that translated into proficiency in cardiac surgery, but he was considered one of the best in central Pennsylvania.

As he walked out of the room, he looked back over his shoulder and said, "Actually, at sixty-three, you're sort of young for this procedure. This should be a walk in the park."

Maybe so, but my guess is that even atheists do a little praying before open-heart surgery. In my case, it was more than a little.

Also, I was grateful that many of my friends from church were praying as well.

Being wheeled into an OR brings on thoughts of mortality, even for a surgeon. Perhaps *especially* for surgeons, since we've seen every crazy crisis imaginable. I was both comforted and somewhat concerned that I knew everyone in the OR on a first-name basis. My concern arose from the fact that I'd screamed at most of them in my days of temper tantrums before coming to faith. Now they seemed to be treating this operation as totally routine, something between a Sunday picnic and a trip to an amusement park. I didn't see it that way. After all, this time, it was *me* on the operating table.

When I awoke from the operation four hours later, I tried to assume the role of patient. But after averaging five or six hundred surgeries a year for the past twenty-eight years, a few hundred of them involving opening patients' chests, I couldn't avoid asking the routine questions any doctor would ask: "How are my vitals?"

I got a nod indicating that they were OK.

I tried another: "How's my chest tube drainage?" Based on the blood loss I'd observed in the chest cases I'd handled, I expected her to say 25 cc's.

"350 cc's this past hour," the nurse answered. "It was 450 the hour before. Looks like it's slowing down. "

Well, I thought, *this is a bit more than post-op oozing.*

The next hour it was 425, then 375, then 450 again. That's not my definition of slowing.

My young, positive-thinking surgeon popped back into the room around four that afternoon. "Professor, you're putting a hit on the blood bank. Surprising—this is the first case that has needed blood in the previous 450."

"Sorry to ruin your series," I mumbled. I vaguely remembered

Felix's morbid disclaimer back when he'd told me I would need surgery: There was a one in thirty chance that I would die from it, but those who did were usually older and had other health problems. I'd thought those were good odds then—not so much anymore.

"See you in the morning," he said. He ordered another unit of blood as he hurried out.

Late-afternoon golf match was my diagnosis.

Good-sized arterial pumper was my next diagnosis. This amount of drainage didn't come from the usual bleeding from the incision or leaking from a vein.

By evening I had the dubious distinction of having had my body's entire blood volume replaced, plus an extra 450 cc's. Now I began recalculating my odds of making it through this.

Receiving that eleventh unit, I sensed that even with all that replacement blood, I was going into shock. The normal metrics of blood pressure were showing only slightly below normal, but the room was becoming blurred. I could feel myself losing consciousness. In over thirty years of surgery, I had never seen a patient in an elective operation lose this much blood. Yes, some of our soldiers in Vietnam pulverized by artillery shell fragments did, but they were twenty years old and began receiving fluids within minutes of the trauma. My trauma was a too-aggressive young surgeon too intent on playing golf.

I later found out that he was also angling for a job with a large pharmaceutical company. I'd have done better with the artillery shell!

My post-op recovery was rapidly becoming a train wreck, and I was living it in slow motion. Because of the fragile blood pressure they could not safely give me pain medication, but pain was the least of my worries.

My mind raced as I considered my alternatives.

One was obvious: death.

Only the most confirmed atheist doesn't pray under these circumstances, and I was at the other end of that spectrum. So I prayed for the usual things: protection for my family, empowerment for them to be able to move on without me … and if God could swing it, my survival!

One of the unusual complications of shock is that patients will occasionally throw up. One of my former partners walked in the door as I threw up, barely missing him. "Don't take that personally," I said. He gave a bad imitation of a laugh.

Behind him was the nurse. I told her, "I don't care what my blood pressure is showing; I know I'm in shock."

"I've already buzzed for Dr. Iams, the doctor on call," she said. Dr. Iams was the hospital's most experienced cardiac surgeon. He was also somewhat cantankerous and frankly so dedicated to his craft that he was rarely aware of the people around him. I had complete confidence in him.

As I continued praying, an unusual thing happened. I felt challenged about what kind of prayer I should be offering.

Was I asking for life? Yes—in fact, *pleading* wouldn't be too strong a word.

For healing? Of course! I had already done that repeatedly.

But something bothered me about those prayers. Eventually it came to me: In effect, I was saying, "I'd rather be here on earth than with you, Jesus."

If I were Jesus, wouldn't I be offended at those prayers? I could imagine him thinking, *I understand you wanting to be with Sally and the kids, but haven't you often said that you loved me more than anything or anybody, and you wanted to be with me for eternity? That could start right now—and yet you're resisting. Who is it you love most? Is it Sally? Your daughter Lynn? Your son Chris? Your grandchildren? Your mother? Is it me, your Savior?*

Those are the kinds of questions I expected to discuss on a Sunday evening, having coffee after a Bible study ... not on the slippery slope to eternity. But this was gut-check time. I had to figure out whom I loved most: God or his creation.

"Hey, doc." It was Frank, the OR orderly. "Can you hop on the gurney?" He chuckled. "This is crazy—I'm usually bringing patients into *your* OR." The crash cart rolled into my room, a few cc's of various meds were squirted into my IV to stabilize my blood pressure, then they rushed me back to the operating room. I was running out of time to deliberate, but I felt that I owed my Maker an answer. This was not a hypothetical Sunday school question. I looked as deeply and honestly as I could at my choices, then answered, *Lord, it is you that I love more than anyone else.*

And yet still, as I was rolled down the hospital corridor, I felt that the matter was unsettled, and I realized that I was being asked another question: *Where, then, do you find your greatest joy? Where do you want to be?*

I knew the answer to that question, and I was pleased to give it—not because it was the right answer, but because it was *my* answer. *My greatest joy is when I'm close to you, Lord!*

Class over!

Just then Renee and Martha, two nurses and old friends from my years in the OR, lifted me onto the OR table, and the crash induction was started with a bolus of sedative, immediately followed by a paralyzing dose of curare, then a choking semi-awake intubation, and finally off to la-la land. The last thing I remember hearing was the scrub nurse saying, "You're in good hands—your anesthesiologist was a former Israeli fighter pilot. No one dies unless he says so!"

Was she talking about my fighter-pilot anesthesiologist ... or my Lord?

I awoke a few hours later, surprisingly alert. It was after midnight. Eighteen hours since the start of my initial operation, a surgery that should have been routine. My experience has been that, when patients start having problems, the problems just keep coming. And I had definitely had problems, enough that I'd had to be rushed back into the OR for a second procedure to save my life. What else would go wrong? Would the next complication be serious enough that my life could not be saved?

I thought of going back to sleep, but the drugs given to reverse the various sedatives and pain meds had created a calm alertness that enabled me to once again address my practical theological question by continuing the prayer I'd begun before surgery.

As I prayed, I became aware that I was not praying alone—I could hear, in fact, a cacophony of voices. But I couldn't make out the words. They sounded like a hailstorm against a tin roof. And yet I somehow knew that all of these voices were praying that I would survive and be healed.

I also had the sense that I was hurtling faster and faster into darkness. Everything was black—it was only sound that filled my awareness, not sight. Was this a test? Was the strength of my faith being challenged? I believed that it was.

The tin-roof sounds of the myriad of voices praying for me cascaded into a frightening roar. I realized that, regardless of what I might want, those voices, those prayers, were carrying the day. They were praying me back toward life.

With that realization, sleep came easily.

A few hours later, I awoke to sun streaming through the window, a memory that remains vivid to this day.

~

When I returned to church, it seemed that over the next few weeks, everyone who attended our church—about five hundred people—mentioned that they had prayed for me during my hospitalization.

When I said, "I know, I could hear it," the most common response was a puzzled smile.

I made no attempt to explain. Who would have believed me? My guess is that you have some reservations even as you read this. But I don't! I was there. I heard the sound of those prayers.

My recovery after the surgery was not 100 percent. During the second surgery, the surgeons had cranked my surgically bisected sternum farther and farther apart until they found, hiding in the apex of my chest behind my lung, the single bleeder—an artery about the size of a drinking straw that was pumping my life away. In doing so, they stretched my brachial plexus, tearing the main nerves of my right arm, partially paralyzing it.

On my six-week follow-up, I asked the surgeon, "Will this paralysis resolve? After all, I am a surgeon. Or at least I was. The ability to use that arm is somewhat important in my trade."

"I don't know," he answered honestly. "I've never seen this brachial plexus palsy complication. I've read about it, but it's so rare it's hard to make a generalization."

There was another question I could have asked—but didn't need to. *What had led him into that hidden alcove of my chest to find the aberrant blood vessel that was pouring my life into a bottle?* Was it his surgical expertise? Clearly God had used him to save my life. But I believed it was the prayers of all those people from the church that guided him and made the crucial difference.

Over the next six weeks, much of the paralysis resolved. But to this day, my right arm remains slightly weaker. And my familial essential tremor, negligible during most of my career, became significantly worse. Most days I'm reminded of it when my handwriting lapses into even worse script than usual, or when I have trouble putting in my contact lenses.

Those are minor inconveniences. A much more serious one: It meant the end of my surgical career. Even so—my life in exchange for a tremor. It seems a pretty good bargain.

PART 4

COMING TO TERMS WITH IMPAIRMENT

CHAPTER 14

From Paranoia
to Alienation

Healing occurs in many ways. Suppose you break your tibia in your lower leg. If you are under fifteen, the doctor makes sure it's straight and puts the leg in a cast, and the fracture heals 99.9 percent of the time. But shatter that tibia in a skiing accident and treatment may require a three-hour operation, a couple of plates, and five to ten screws. Still, if the skin hasn't been torn open by the injury, you have better than a 95 percent chance of uneventful healing.

But if you break your tibia in a high-speed motorcycle accident—with skin ripped open, both the tibia and fibula fractured, greasy gravel ground into the wound, and the tibial artery ruptured—healing may well require multiple operations, and you face the possibility of losing your leg.

$\backsim$

My uncle was an Army doctor in America's deadliest single World War II battle, with 19,000 killed and 89,000 wounded— the Battle of the Bulge. Like so many who survived, he never healed from the psychic trauma. Alcohol slaked his pain. He didn't die in that fiercest of battles, but afterward he died little by little, day after day, drink by drink. His experience has been repeated, with variations, by many other returning war veterans and by many professional football players and boxers who are recovering from traumatic brain injuries—and by many who, like me, suffer TBIs through other means.

For twenty-six months after my ski slope accident and its aftermath, which I detailed in part 1, I still didn't know I was impaired. The organ that should have told me I wasn't performing adequately, my brain, wasn't working normally.

What were some of my symptoms—even if I didn't recognize them as such at the time?

I began mentally *compulsively replaying conversations,* "flashbacks" of prior meetings. This, I later learned, is typical of those with post-concussion syndrome.

And all of that compulsive review was processed through a screen of *paranoia.* Do you remember the bad joke about paranoids: Someone says "Good morning!" to a person with paranoia, and the paranoid wanders away mumbling, "Where does he get off telling me it's a good morning? I'll be the judge of that! Who does he think he is, anyway?" Sadly, that stale joke had too much truth when applied to my state of mind. And some of my board members at CURE were on the receiving end of my cynicism.

In an attempt to compensate, I became *hypervigilant.* I compulsively rechecked things, something I'd never done before the TBI.

Depression! I had never been subject to bouts of hopeless melancholy, so I didn't know what to make of it. I interpreted my depression, although at the time I thought of it more as simple sadness, as natural for someone leaving something that had consumed his whole life for sixteen years. And when I say "whole life," that was literally true. My travel schedule, about 150,000 to 200,000 miles per year, precluded regular church attendance, and with it, the friendships associated with active participation in a local church. I had no more time for golf, therefore no more golfing buddies. I never found time to see my former partners from my years of orthopedic surgery.

I was now alone. I was desperately lonely and angry about it! But I didn't diagnose it at the time as a symptom of a damaged brain. I thought it was just natural to feel that way in my circumstances.

And I lost what I had always considered my core attribute: optimism. I was, for the first time in my life, clinically depressed. I don't remember times of personal despondency before that, not ever, even during my year in Vietnam. Sure, while I was there I had missed my wife and two baby girls and grieved over the maimed soldiers who were regular visitors to our hospital. But that was appropriate sorrow, not pathologic despair.

I developed *insomnia*. I still can't believe it! Previously I could sleep in a plane, a train, a doctor's lounge, a moving car (not while driving, fortunately), while waiting for a haircut ... well, you get the idea. After my concussion, I awoke about 3:00 or 4:00 a.m. to rehash all the real and imagined calamities in my life. The exasperation of being unable to control these destructive emotions continued to escalate into a fury. I found myself screaming at God in the middle of my morning walks with my dog as I tried, ineffectually, to pray!

Another hallmark of TBIs is *substance abuse*. Mine happened seamlessly. When I was active as a surgeon, I never touched alcohol in any form unless I was confident that I would have no need to care for patients. When I left orthopedic surgery to enter the business world, aka the realm of three-martini lunches and a bottle of wine with dinner, I quickly learned that the successful CEO was a sober CEO. But after the TBI, substance abuse slipped up on me slowly and stealthily—and because the organ I needed to make that self-diagnosis, my brain, was impaired, I missed it. The *occasional* glass with dinner became two, then two and a half, *every* night. Doesn't sound like much? I became accustomed to two glasses, still feeling sober, but as that increased, even just an extra half glass, I could sense the difference in my mental functioning from that extra amount. But if I thought about it at all, it was only, *I have no patients to worry about, no potential life-changing decision to make for my company—so why not?*

I began to look forward to that glass of wine each evening … and the second … and …

I never had an accident while driving. Never missed a meeting or a phone call. Never drank alone or before dinner. Perhaps I don't even qualify as an alcoholic; perhaps I was just being hypersensitive because my father and grandfather were alcoholics. But I couldn't really tell, because my brain was compromised.

So in desperation, sensing my mental impairment, I began "exercising" my brain with the currently popular online programs: Lumosity and then BrainHQ. I thought of it as the poor man's cognitive therapy program.

Perhaps the greatest difference in the medical understanding of our bodies in the years since I went to medical school is the concept of the plasticity of our brains. No longer do we shrug our shoulders and accept that our brains gradually deteriorate. We now know that, even in our eighth decade, we can "exercise" our brains to make them more nimble and slow the effects of aging.

After a couple months of regular Lumosity brain exercises, each session lasting about forty-five minutes, I noticed that my daily brain test scores also included a cumulative record. It was expressed as my performance compared to others over seventy-five.

I was in the 35th percentile! Said another way, two out of three in my age group had better brain function than I. As a younger man, before my TBI, I had tested out in the 95th percentile in mental acuity; post-TBI, I had fallen to this functional but unaccustomed level.

Sad to say, one of the other symptoms of TBI is suicide. Estimates now suggest that at least 10 percent and perhaps as high as 20 percent of combat soldiers with TBI will eventually find relief by taking their own life.

Logically, leaving CURE, as emotionally difficult as it was, should have made a positive change in my TBI symptoms because it eliminated a significant source of stress and conflict. Unfortunately, that didn't turn out to be true—or if it was, the improvement must have been minor. There was certainly no improvement in depression or anxiety. Nor self-blame. The negative self-talk, if anything, increased. And insomnia was still a nightly ritual.

But I couldn't have explained that in anything approaching the level of lucidity I'm employing here. I knew only that I was confused, angry, and unhappy. I couldn't have told you why, or even explained my symptoms coherently.

Since one of CURE's founding principles was combining prayer and spiritual healing with the traditional practice of medical healing, and since over my years with CURE I had experienced success when approaching healing that way (as evidenced by the stories I've related in this book), you'd think I might have understood that dynamic and attempted to enlist prayer as an avenue to physical and spiritual healing.

I didn't. I simply wasn't thinking that clearly. When I needed to be healed, sadly, I was slow to turn to the real Source.

But then, I wasn't the same person who had founded CURE. Like so many who experience head trauma, my reality had changed.

Had I been functioning at a higher cognitive level, I would have clearly seen, in those days after I was forced to step away from CURE, that my brain injury in March of 2011 had become a pivotal turning point in my life. My internist had assured me, six weeks after my concussion, that I was OK, and I'd felt, erroneously, that I'd "dodged a bullet." But 50 percent of those who have a traumatic brain injury of my severity die within the next seventy-two to ninety-two hours from the traumatic interstitial contusion and subdural hematoma. Complete recovery occurs in only 20 to 30 percent of patients.

〜

Soon there was more stress. Although it was far from clear to me for all of the reasons I just explained, the changes in my emotional and cognitive abilities and tendencies were creating serious problems between me and the rest of the team at CURE—especially the board members. I had already stepped down from the presidency of the ministry and was now just a board member. Even though that was a reduced role from what I'd held previously, it was precious to me.

It was also in jeopardy. Sally and I received a call from her closest friend on the board asking for a meeting. We made the two-and-a-half-hour drive to Philadelphia, sat down in our friend's hotel suite, and within five minutes were told that we—both of us—had been unanimously voted off the board. We were being given the opportunity to resign.

Sally and I were both stunned and confused. We had given up so much to start and nurture CURE. It occurred to me that whatever had gone wrong between me and the rest of the board, many who were longtime friends, it was somehow connected with my TBI. Except for the chairman, the board, along with my coworkers at CURE, knew nothing about my brain injury. Paranoids—me for example, operating with an impaired brain—don't tell those who they believe are enemies anything. But then, they don't know there is anything to tell!

Was this a vicious cycle? Was the TBI I'd suffered to blame for my alienation from the ministry I had founded? And was the emotional and psychological stress of that alienation now to blame for the continuation of my post-concussion syndrome?

CHAPTER 15

FINAL HEALING

Our dismissal from the board was followed by long hours of dissecting everything that had happened leading up to it—not surprising, given the paranoia and obsessive behavior caused by my TBI. Since I was too impaired to see the dysfunction of my own daily mental functions, I certainly couldn't read the emotional reactions of others with any degree of certainty. But some things were clear even to me. How could I miss, for instance, that I could no longer tee my golf ball because my right hand shook so badly? The mild "familial tremor" I had discovered in medical school had become a disabling, shuddering quiver. On what should have been a pleasant day of golf a few weeks earlier, a board member had offered to place my ball on the tee after I had tried, unsuccessfully, several times—eventually even trying it with two hands.

My response to that well-intentioned offer was, "I'll quit before I'll do that!" growled through clenched teeth. That summed up my emotional status, and not just on the golf course.

The symptoms resulting from my TBI were unpleasant and constant. So how can one treat them? There is no surgery that can change the damage to the substance of the brain. Surgery can remove problems such as blood clots, tumors, and foreign bodies like bullets. The brain can then heal, at least to some extent. In my case, immediate surgery would have decompressed my sub-dural hematoma. But it probably would not have been helpful for the contusion of the brain substance, unless it had been done at the very beginning. It wasn't, because at that time I hadn't real-ized the nature of my injury.

There are multiple drugs used for the chronic symptoms of TBIs, mainly antidepressants, but the results are underwhelming. Cognitive therapy has about the same success rate, or more cor-rectly, failure rate, as drugs.

But I had always seen my glass as half full. Even though my optimism had been thrown off balance by my injury, the habits of a lifetime are hard to break, and throughout the years, my question has never been "Can we?" but rather "How do we?"—how do we get the patient healed, or the company refinanced, or the problem solved?

And I had something else: fifteen years of memories of the tiny heroes I've written about in the chapters of this book and many more, those patients who were paralyzed, who had crooked legs or deformed hands, most of them children. They too had faced long odds and endured painful surgeries and recoveries, some having lived in pain for years. And yet they faced those poor odds with hope and a smile.

What was the common factor in their recoveries? They had all prayed, their parents had prayed, and their friends had prayed. They possessed, and were surrounded by, solid belief that prayer could change their lives—and, yes, an understanding and accep-tance that prayer didn't result in healing in all cases. Why? Only God knows!

So I joined those thousands of our patients who had appealed to God. I begged, beseeched, implored, and cajoled my Savior for relief from my personality changes: lethargy, memory problems, insomnia, restlessness, irritability, apathy, depression, trouble concentrating, and anxiety. And … did I mention the problem with my memory?

Oh, yes—and anger. Lots and lots of anger. I mean, really *real* anger!

No answer.

And I prayed, and prayed, and prayed.

Nothing!

I continued praying.

Still nothing.

More prayer.

Nothing!

Zero!

Often, perhaps most of the time, rage would rush in before I could even complete my prayers, crushing them.

Would listening to spiritual music drown out the fury? No, that often made it burst out with even greater venom. But I kept trying it anyway.

I confess that before I committed my life to Christ, I was subject to fits of anger, of uncontrolled, throw-something fury. It was an integral part of who I was. Only Sally was safe from my spontaneous tirades. But God had healed me of that!

Now, in the wake of my TBI, I had regressed and gotten even worse. No one was safe from my rages—except, once again, Sally.

Now I raged not just against the darkness but against the anger itself!

Now, in my pathological state, I believed, *I have enemies!*

I had never had an enemy before.

Were some of the CURE board members my enemies?

In Vietnam, a sniper once shot at me as I walked to our ER. It missed my head by a few inches and blew a hole in the Quonset hut behind me; I collected the bullet. Even though he tried to kill me, that shooter wasn't my *personal* enemy. However he understood or misunderstood the United States, our nation was his enemy, and therefore, even though he and I had never met and knew nothing about each other, I was his enemy.

Love your enemies! I'd read that command a thousand times. But I'd always skimmed right over it, thinking, *wonderful sentiment—but since I have no enemies, it's nothing I need to concentrate on.*

Now things were different. *Jesus,* I prayed, *when you talked about "enemies" in the Sermon on the Mount, did you really mean for us to love those who set out to destroy us? Those who succeed? Just how seriously do you want me to take this "forgiving my enemies"?*

How seriously did you take it? I asked him.

"To die for," he whispered back, his voice raspy and urgent from the cross.

My ears reverberated with his intensity.

And it was of course true. He had died on the cross not just for his friends, not just for those who loved him, but equally for his enemies.

I was aiming at a much lower target than loving my enemies. I just needed to believe that I could trust my friends. And I was trying to get a handle on my rage—and not doing a very good job. In fact, I was losing the battle. It was all I could do to keep my fury from destroying me and those I loved.

Well, one blessing in all of the emotional noise: My prayer life improved, even interrupted as it often was by my rages. Early mornings, walking my dog through our forest, quiet except for the hooting of our resident owl, Christian hymns blasting from my iPhone, included pleading to God to lift this burden of suffocating anger.

That command kept echoing in my head: "Love your enemies." It urged me to go far beyond just recovering, beyond just going back to the way I had been. Initially I'd been pleading with God to quiet my rage. Once that happened, I reasoned I could work on forgiveness ... although frankly, I couldn't imagine that happening.

Now I realized I had set the bar far too low. Jesus called me to *love* my enemies. Did it matter that, possibly, I saw them as enemies only because my brain was functioning at perhaps only a third of its former power? I *perceived* them as enemies, and therefore, to me, they were enemies.

I made tiny steps of healing. I might go a full minute of praying before the rage intruded. I would sense improvement, then suddenly fall off the cliff back into hopelessness and rage.

Would I be cursed with this anger for the rest of my life?

One afternoon, standing in our bedroom, I cried out to God as I had countless times: "Do you realize how many times I've asked you for healing? And I'm going to keep on asking ... and asking ..."

Through clenched teeth I whispered, "Father, I know you are the God of miracles. I've seen them in the children you've healed. Now *I* need to be healed! Only you can do it. All I can do is ask, and keep on asking. And I will! I will!" I shouted.

Exhausted, I continued in a soft whisper. "Jesus, you have challenged me to love my enemies, and you know there are some people I despise now. Spirit, many years ago you came to me when I was frustrated and lost, and you baptized me. Only you can bring healing to me now. I ask, I plead, I challenge you in love to work a miracle in me. I've seen you do it before, and I need you to again. Please, please—heal me!"

I sobbed quietly.

Then, almost imperceptibly, the intimate, tangible presence of the Spirit of God enveloped me. A warmth, an ineffable sense of actual physical presence, embraced me, suffusing every cell of my body, a fusion of the corporal and spiritual, his Holy Spirit.

The sensation was unmistakable. I knew that I'd been changed. Every cell in me was different. Simply hearing his voice would have been a miracle, but what I felt was even better: I experienced his presence.

I don't know how long it lasted, but I cherished every second. When it was over, I knew that for me, it was also a beginning.

I knew that I could now do what Jesus had commanded me to do: I could love those who I'd believed had mistreated me, and whom I'd treated as enemies. I knew that, besides the rage, I had also been healed of the other sequelae of the traumatic brain injury: the anxiety, the depression, the insomnia, the irritability.

"I've been healed," I said, shaking my head in amazement. "It's so hard to accept—but I'm sure of it."

Through the power of the Holy Spirit, on October 19, nineteen months after my brain injury and subdural hematoma, the uncontrolled rage that had possessed me for months was gone.

And I knew it wouldn't return.

Only through this direct touch of Jesus and the imparting of the power of the Holy Spirit to overcome the emotional effects of my injury would I now be able to follow his command: *Love your enemies.*

Loving our enemies, I now saw, is not about *us* and *them*. It is about us and our Savior. It is a way to be drawn into the presence of Jesus in a tangible way.

This insight isn't uniquely mine. I just hadn't seen it before. Paul, that irascible, opinionated, uptight, not-so-lovable guy, understood it when he wrote what is sometimes called the biblical "hymn of love"—a how-to set of instructions delivered as a lyric poem. My mother had insisted I memorize these verses when I was a child. Instructions to love not just fellow believers, not just friends and family, but, astoundingly, to love our enemies—even, as in my case, those I may only *think* are my enemies:

> Love is patient,
> Love is kind,
> Love is not envying,
> Love does not boast,
> Love is not proud,
> Love is not rude,
> Love is not self-seeking,
> Love is not easily angered,
> Love does not record wrongs,
> Love does not delight in evil,
> For
> Love rejoices in truth,
> Love protects,
> Love trusts,
> Love hopes,
> Love perseveres. (based on 1 Cor. 13:4–7)

Two thousand years later, through the power of the Holy Spirit, this passage is still true, and I now knew it in a way I'd never understood as a child.

It had been twenty-nine years since, in Malawi, I had

witnessed God's miracle of healing Lewis. During that time, God, through the organization he'd enabled Sally and me to birth, had physically healed more than a hundred thousand children and brought eternal life to about the same number, along with their parents, sisters, and brothers.

And now he had lavished his curative love on me!

How could I not be joyful?

He had healed even me!

⤷

Now I could get on with my life! I could speak. Better yet, I could manifest how God had brought healing into my life.

I was honored by my alma mater, the Orthopedic Department of the Medical College of Wisconsin, and asked to give a speech at their annual graduation ceremony. It was a reminder that maybe I wasn't as worthless as I'd recently felt.

A short time later, another talk, this time to a couple hundred retirees. I enjoyed speaking about our work, about the children, and about the God of healing. I could breathe life into the story of a child unable to walk who had now been healed because I too could now walk, upright, resilient, as I sensed God's power. Perhaps I'd forgotten far more than I could remember, but I still had his help in telling how my healing was also from a post-traumatic, life-crushing depression, and that I was now on a journey of physical and spiritual healing. Now I could speak of God's healing because it hadn't happened just to my patients—it had happened to me.

How far my brain's plasticity would take me toward healing I would just have to see, trusting and patiently waiting while doing my part with regular "brain exercises."

Sure, in preparing to speak, I needed to remind myself what had happened during the events I wanted to speak about by referring to prior correspondence and my old Day-Timers to fill in the blank mental spaces I could no longer recall.

My healing was like that of a bad tibial fracture. I could now walk on it, but I still had a painful limp. I expected that soon I'd be running. Not as fast as I'd done in my prime, but then who can? Heck, I was fast approaching eighty! A brisk jog would now be the acceptable norm!

At a talk in Chicago, I mentioned the 100 billion neurons in the average brain. I knew that I'd lost a few hundred thousand, maybe even a billion neurons or two on that ski slope. That would leave 98 or 99 billion still working well—as did the talk!

But like nearly all traumatic brain injury patients, I was uneasy talking about my injury because when I did, I routinely heard, "You're just imagining this. You're fine. That was a great talk you just gave!"

If I'd broken my leg and walked with a limp, then others would have understood the nature of my injury and the effect it had on me. Brain injuries—not so much.

Other speaking engagements followed. I just had to tell about the God of healing and how that healing may take many forms.

Not all TBI patients find healing. The high suicide rates of those who've suffered a TBI show that much more needs to be done.

⤿

Months later, as I was standing in front of my computer, a crushing substernal pain exploded in my chest—the classic symptom of a heart attack. Even an orthopedic surgeon knows those.

I waited a few minutes. The overpowering pain increased. One of the fatal complications that can occur quickly in an ischemic heart is cardiac arrhythmia, a futile heart fluttering rather than the rhythmic filling and emptying of normal heart function. A variant of that is fibrillation, the very rapid, partial filling and emptying of the heart. If that developed, I would likely die before I made it to the ER.

As calmly as one contemplating his own death could, I walked up the steps from my office and said to Sally, "I'm having severe substernal chest pain. Take me to the ER."

Sally's years of nursing experience told her just what needed to be done. Without another word, we walked slowly to the garage, then drove quickly but not over the speed limit to the ER.

Eleven minutes after I'd first spoken to Sally, I calmly told the ER clerk, "I'm having a heart attack. I have now had about seventeen minutes of crushing substernal pain."

She nonchalantly nodded for an orderly to bring a wheelchair and I was soon on an examining table, EKG leads being applied in all the appropriate places and a young resident asking the usual questions.

The pain continued for another forty-five minutes. After a shot of who-knows-what, it subsided.

Four hours later, having obtained the opinions of multiple doctors, I lay on the X-ray table, the cardiologist standing nearby, as the two of us viewed the monitor displaying the images of the three arterial cardiac bypass grafts that had been inserted sixteen years earlier. Even an orthopedist could diagnose that each of them was still doing its job of delivering the normal flow of blood.

But the test also confirmed that my chest pain had indeed been cardiogenic. For each time a bolus of dye was injected, it temporarily replaced the blood normally nourishing that section of the heart. That reproduced exactly the pain symptoms I'd just been experiencing. So it was *spasms* of my arteries, not occlusions that had caused my chest pain. Spasms caused by the frustrations emanating from my traumatic brain injury, made worse by the "shunning" Sally and I were experiencing from former coworkers and board members after we had been dismissed from CURE's board.

Who knew that shunning could be fatal?

So I didn't need more medication. I needed to continue my journey of healing from the effects of being ostracized by those I'd worked and served with.

Perhaps I could somehow overcome that also.

❧

Soon thereafter I received a surprise: an invitation to an eightieth-year surprise birthday party, at the CURE office, for our close friend who was also the first assistant I'd hired at CURE. The invitation came from a mutual friend who didn't work at CURE. So most of the party's attendees would be employees of CURE—those same people who had been told to shun us these past three years and had been doing just that.

I saw this as a next step on our road of healing.

Sally saw it as another opportunity to be humiliated.

Would the party be enjoyable? No way to tell ahead of time. But the party's guest of honor was one of our oldest friends, and allowing those who refused our company to continue to control our lives was no longer acceptable. Yes, attending the party could backfire. It could set us back. But it also offered another step up our rung of healing.

The party would be held at CURE's new offices. A few friends and relatives not associated with CURE would also be there. So even if shunned by those at CURE, we could still talk with the others we would know.

This would be no tiny step—it would be a giant one. The only question was, forward or backward?

For three years, we had heard not one word from the board members of CURE. Some of those board members, I suspected, would be at the surprise birthday party. How many? Only a few? Several? Maybe none?

So be it. It would be awkward. As Sally pointed out, it might mean having a back turned to us as I extended an outstretched hand. Perhaps even having a former friend walk out rather than acknowledge our presence.

As painful as the experience might turn out to be, I realized that I was experiencing, and had been experiencing since the frustrations surrounding my "firing" from CURE, the terrible frustrations that all or nearly all TBI patients experience. Those veterans, for instance, who return to the States after being injured during combat, perhaps from a roadside bomb in the Middle East, and find themselves thinking over and over again of family and friends who before deployment seemed so loving and supportive, but now ... *Why don't they understand?* The problem might be more in the TBI patient's perception than in actuality, but when you're on the inside looking out, that's not a distinction you can recognize.

My TBI experience was undoubtedly more like the "sniffles" compared to the "pneumonia" of injuries imparted by terrorist bombs. But many of those GIs, like me, returned stateside with no telltale limp. No scarred face. No artificial leg. And without those outward signs, people tend to disbelieve you're actually still suffering from a debilitating injury, in this case one that affects your behavior, your emotions, your perceptions.

On the afternoon of the surprise party, we arrived about forty-five minutes after it began. There were surprisingly few cars in the parking lot.

Oh my, I thought. *They gave a party and nobody came! Maybe that's why we were invited. Or worse, maybe the others knew we were invited and decided not to come.*

It felt a little eerie. Sally put her arm through mine and clutched me in a death grip. Where was everybody?

It turned out that most of the guests had parked behind the building to make sure the guest of honor was surprised.

My stomach twisted into a knot as we approached the building and I saw, standing by the door, a close friend of the CURE president who had given us the boot. *Has he heard that we're coming and he's here to stop us? This may be the shortest visit of my life. We may not even get past the door.*

As he lifted his hand, I thought my worst fears were about to be realized!

What a dumb idea I'd had. We weren't even going to get in the front door. He was going to hold us back. I hoped it wouldn't get ugly.

Instead, he grasped my hand and pumped it. "So, so glad you made it."

Right behind him was one of my former secretaries. She shook my hand, gave Sally a hug, and pulled us into the entrance hall. "I'm so pleased you're here! Are you OK? You know ... being here? Does it feel too awkward?"

Before I could answer, the tiny dynamo who focused on CURE Kids threw her arms around me and began gushing about her new house.

I never got to hear the end of her description, because another former secretary who had been promoted numerous times in the intervening years eagerly joined the conversation to tell how she and her new husband had just barely managed to afford a house that "even has a view of the river!"

Kyalo, our first African hire, grabbed my hand as he asked about my son-in-law Jim. "Tell him how grateful I am for all he taught me." Then he was swept away by the ever-enlarging crowd that surrounded us.

A friend of twenty-plus years (although we hadn't seen each other in the past three years because of the shunning) brought me up to date about his daughters and the number of grandchildren he'd been blessed with. The smile never left his face.

Mark, Joel, Jody, Cathy ... they kept coming.

Vic, now permanently back from Afghanistan, and his wife mentioned that he'd found a new lawyer who could help him get his medical license reinstated. "She has done this with other docs, and she's quite optimistic."

His wife kept nodding, her smile lighting the room. I leaned closer and said in a stage whisper, "I so admire you for honoring your wedding vows: *better or worse, sickness or health.* Your husband is one of my heroes."

"Mine too!" she said.

It went on ... and on!

Sally and I had agreed that we would stay only a short time, and after forty-five minutes, we began to head toward the door. But the way was blocked by a man at least half a head taller than me. He looked vaguely familiar. I couldn't decide if the look on his face was a smile or the grimace of one expecting pain or about to deliver it.

"Hi!" he said a little too loudly. "Greg!" He shook his head nervously as if that hadn't been what he'd meant to say. "We met at my parents' house many years ago." As if starting over, he said, "My name is Greg, and this is my wife, Julie." He put his free arm around the woman beside him.

All this time, he hadn't stopped shaking my hand.

"I know everyone wants to talk with you, but we wondered ..." He paused. "We wondered if you would be willing to come to our home for dinner."

By this time, I had placed him. It had been his mother who had delivered the crushing news that Sally and I were being fired. *And given that, you want Sally and me to come to your house?*

I realized now why his expression was uneasy. He was afraid that we would turn him down.

"Sally and I would be pleased to," I answered without hesitation.

He exhaled with relief. "That would be great. Just great! We live—"

"I remember where you live. It's just a few blocks from our house," I said.

His wife nodded, smiling.

As we left the building, I was ecstatic. I was just turning to Sally to tell her so when another former secretary came running across the parking lot. "I didn't have a chance to tell you ... well, how much working with you meant to me," she said, grasping my hand in both of hers. "When I would ask you a question, not only would you give me the answer, you would explain what other alternatives might be ... and why this was the best answer. And if I asked what seemed like a dumb question, you would always tell me that it wasn't a dumb question at all."

She squeezed my hand. "I just wanted to say again how much

it meant to me … you know … the way you treated me. Thanks so much!"

I felt a soft afterglow as we drove out of the parking lot. What had caused this dramatic change in the attitudes of my former coworkers? Neither Sally nor I had done anything different. But from this point on, I would remember June 29 as life changing. We had risked further shunning, but it hadn't happened. Just the reverse. We had been showered in love.

⌒

Our reconnection with friends and loved ones on June 29, 2016, was a seminal event on the road to my recovery, a once-in-a-life-time experience. But another would take place on Friday, January 6, 2017.

CURE had a twentieth anniversary banquet. Sally and I were invited, but the invitation came with a caveat: I was not to say anything from the podium.

Given that caveat, Sally and I debated whether we should attend. I felt compelled to thank those 150 or so people who had been so important to CURE's success, and I would need to have a few minutes at the podium to do that. If I couldn't do that, should I go at all? Wouldn't it be an insult to those who had worked so hard and so sacrificially to make CURE a reality and to bring healing to those 150,000 children around the world if the founder of the ministry was there and yet didn't say a word of thanks or appreciation? On the other hand, would it be worse if I didn't come at all, didn't shake their hands, put my arms around them, whisper words of thanks?

In the end, we decided to go. We'd been told to arrive at 7:00 p.m. Nearly everyone was already there by that time, and to our amazement, as we took our seats, we were surrounded by friends and former employees giving a pleasantly suffocating mixture of hugs and handshakes. We hadn't been at all sure how we would be received, and this expression of appreciation, freely given, was overwhelming.

At dinner's end, the awarding of plaques to those with long-term employment with CURE began. Then my first resident, Theuri, gave what amounted to a twenty-minute eulogy of Sally's and my contribution to birthing CURE. With the "no speaking" caveat whispered once more, we were called to the podium, where Sally and I were given a booklet that had numerous messages from those whom we had worked with during the sixteen years we had labored for CURE.

How could I not thank those workers, at whatever level, who had made CURE the success that it has become?

I needed to take this last step of healing! I took the three steps to the microphone. The floodlights made it impossible for me to recognize anyone.

I had to bend down to talk, since Theuri is only five foot six. I thanked him ... I thanked them ... I thanked God.

But I needed to do one more thing. I needed to tell them how CURE really got started. It wasn't when we built our first hospital in Kenya.

It wasn't even when we returned to Africa after my time as president of Kirschner, the orthopedic manufacturing company.

It had been in 1990, when I asked God if I should leave my career as an orthopedic surgeon, as chairman of our church board, as professor of orthopedic surgery at Penn State's medical school, and as a member of the leadership in our church to run a failing orthopedic manufacturing company. I told them how I'd answered God's unambiguously clear calling to, of all things, save a dying public company whose stock had fallen from $28 to $4 and was in the beginning of bankruptcy.

On that occasion, after a surprisingly short time of prayer, I'd answered yes.

Seven years later, those "worthless" stock options I'd been given in place of an appropriate salary were worth about $30 million. That was the seed that enabled CURE to begin healing children spiritually and medically.

I challenged them to simply say yes when God asks ... even when you don't know why he is asking.

And then we were done.

A standing ovation erupted. It went on ... and on!

Then came another half hour of picture taking and hand shaking, seemingly with nearly every person there.

I couldn't help but think of my post-concussion syndrome and how it had derailed my relationship with CURE.

Like CURE, God specializes in healing. He is the source of that healing!

And if we are faithful in prayer, that healing will continue—in our own lives, within CURE, and in the countries around the world where CURE is active.

Healing, both medical and spiritual, is the wish of our triune God.

That was my wish as well.

He did!

He does!

He will!

THE FINAL STEP

I CELEBRATED MY EIGHTIETH BIRTHDAY IN A "SMASHING" way—at the Royal Ascot, the three-hundred-year-old racecourse founded by Queen Anne. Pageantry! Excitement! And yes, the Queen was there—although not, I'm sure, for my birthday.

As momentous as that celebration was, however, Sally and I celebrated the milestone of my eightieth with something much, much more important. Saying yes to God once again, we decided to start a new company.

It's called The Final Step. The idea sprang from a visit I'd made to India fifteen years before while exploring the possibility of building one of our children's hospitals in Hyderabad, in south-central India. There was a unique local company that processed hospital transcription. Not transcription for Indian hospitals—rather, they serviced American hospitals. Taking advantage of the time difference, dictation done at day's end in the States, usually patient histories and physical exams, would arrive via the magic of the Internet at the start of the day in Hyderabad. The company's workers were much less expensive than Stateside options and the quality every bit as good.

The Final Step operates similarly. Technically, it's a BPO, a business processing outsourcing business. We have trained a cadre of partially disabled Kenyans, some of whom were operated on in our hospital in Kijabe, to do these First World jobs while in the Third World.

They work well below the cost of similar labor in First World countries but significantly above wages in Kenya. We anticipate that we can find similar tasks that can be outsourced to our former patients elsewhere in Africa, South America, or Asia.

The United Nations reports that 90 percent of the 238,000,000 people with disabilities in the world are unemployed. Some of these are the very people treated at CURE hospitals for birth defects, crooked spines, or any of dozens of childhood abnormalities.

It isn't hard to imagine what they would say if asked what a job would mean in their lives. Might they use their own language's version of words like: *wonderful, marvelous, phenomenal*—perhaps even *miraculous* or *supernatural*?

Am I too old for this?

Don't bet on it!

But perhaps a more important question is: Would I have the time and availability to attack this important opportunity, one with the potential to be life-changing for so many, if I were still CEO of CURE—if, in other words, my brain injury and the resulting changes in my personality and behavior had never happened? And the answer is: Probably not.

Who can know the mind of God?